ENGLISH NARROW GAUGE ALBUM
VOLUME ONE

Title page: The Torrington & Marland Railway, built in Devon to carry clay, featured the innovative viaduct designs of John Barraclough Fell and was worked efficiently as an industrial railway, but succumbed to a standard gauge conversion to enable wider local political objectives to be served. The Avonside Engineering Co. 0-6-0ST *Avonside*, Works No. 1428 of 1901, places some wagons at the Watergate siding. [John Alsop collection]

This page: The Leek & Manifold is fondly remembered for the magnificent scenery it ran through, Thor's Cave, the beautiful large steam engines, the ornate and unusually-liveried carriages and the intriguing transporter wagons. Engineer Everard Calthrop designed a most practical narrow gauge solution but, whilst it was adopted for the Manifold Valley, it was probably too late to secure long life for the narrow gauge in Britain. [Neil Parkhouse collection]

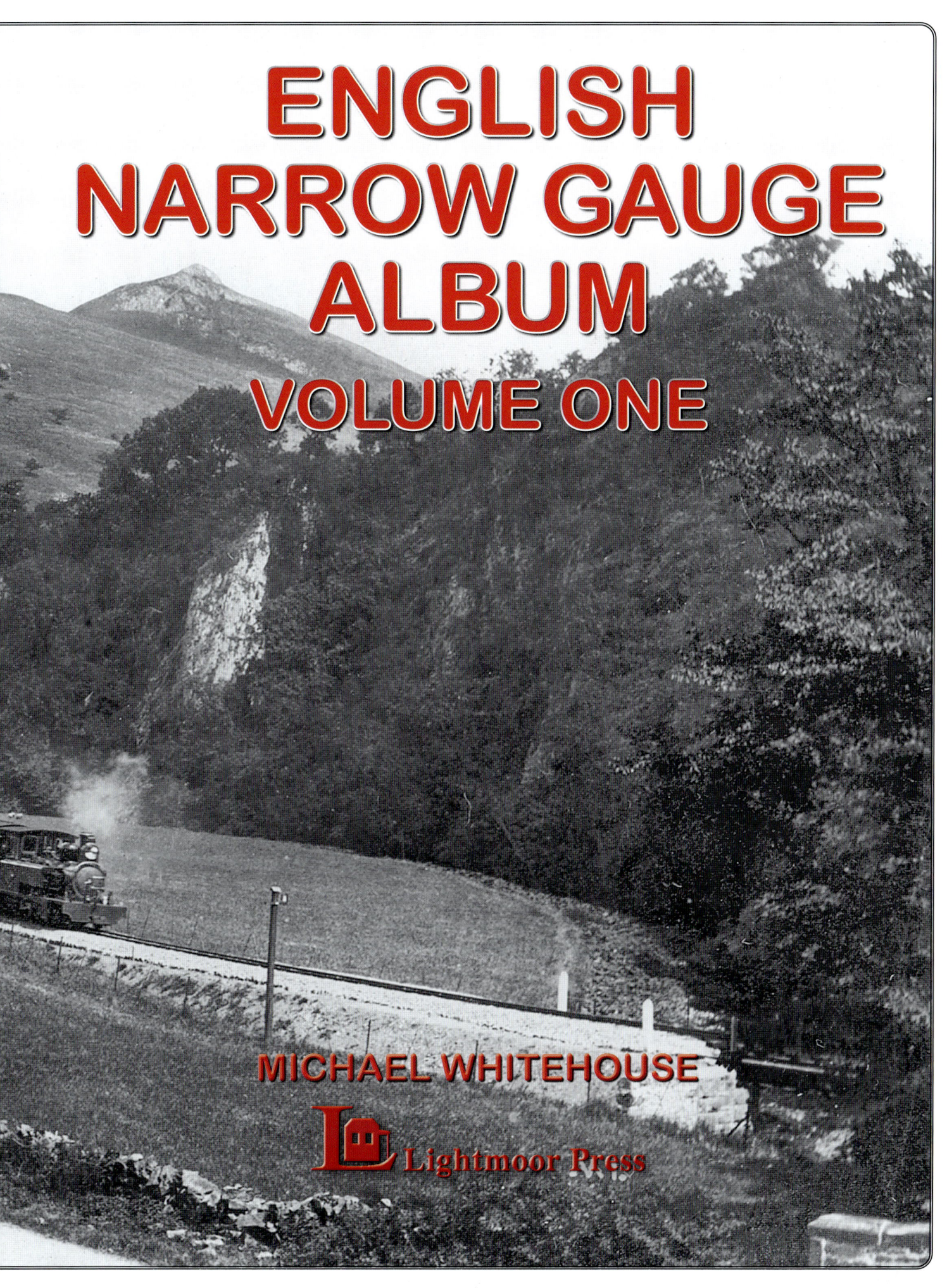

ENGLISH NARROW GAUGE ALBUM

VOLUME ONE

MICHAEL WHITEHOUSE

Lightmoor Press

ABOUT THE AUTHOR

Michael Whitehouse has always been interested in narrow gauge railways, at home and abroad. In his childhood, he was largely brought up on the Talyllyn Railway in the 1950s on summer holidays, when his father was Secretary to the Talyllyn Railway Preservation Society. In university holidays, he volunteered on the Festiniog Railway at Boston Lodge Works and occasionally fired the summer high season trains. Later he became a qualified fireman on the Welshpool & Llanfair Railway. He is a commercial finance lawyer by profession and has advised on many complex railway projects in Britain, Europe, Africa and Asia. In his legal capacity, he volunteered to assist the regeneration of the Welsh Highland Railway by the Festiniog Railway. He joined the core reconstruction team and later became Chairman of its construction company and then the Festiniog Railway Company itself.

The Southwold Railway in East Anglia was conceived to fill a local need, the town having been ignored by the Great Eastern Railway, which considered greater returns more likely from nearby Lowestoft. The Southwold was well designed and run in accordance with Rapier's light railway principles discussed in this book, but succumbed to road transport after the outbreak of the First World War as an outmoded system. [John Alsop collection]

ACKNOWLEDGMENTS

Grateful thanks to the people below for their willing help in supporting production, providing pictures and checking proofs. If you are interested in finding out more detail about any of the railways featured in this book, please consider reading the books listed below.

John Adams, John Alsop, R.A.H. Baxter, British Railways, Roger Carpenter, Laurie A. Cooksey [*Rye & Camber Tramway*], John Cosford, W.J.K Davies [*Light Railways*], Gordon Edgar, Liz Fuller, Martin Fuller, Robert Gratton [*The Leek & Manifold Valley Light Railway*], Robert J. Harley [*Birmingham Tramways*], Philip Hindley, Robert Humm, Industrial Railway Society, Paul Ingham, Alan A. Jackson [*Volk's Railways Brighton*], Peter Johnson, M.J.T. Lewis [*Pentewan Railway*], London & North Western Railway Society, Michael Messenger [*North Devon Clay*], National Railway Museum, Neil Parkhouse, Andrew Neale, Peter Paye [*The Southwold Railway*], Keith Pearson [*Fell Mountain Railways*], P.J.G. Ransom [*Narrow Gauge Steam*], R.P. Richards, L.T.C. Rolt [*Hunslet Hundred*], Richard Rolt, Mark Smithers [*18 Inch Gauge Steam Railways*], Statfold Barn Railway, Ted Talbot [*Crewe Works Narrow Gauge System*], Dave Waldren.

CONTENTS

Acknowledgements .... page 4
INTRODUCTION .... page 7
1 MINIMUM GAUGE .... page 17
2 A CORNISH ENGINEMAN'S VIEW:
  THE PENTEWAN RAILWAY .... page 41
3 OUTPACED BY DEMAND:
  THE TORRINGTON & MARLAND RAILWAY .... page 55
4 A MISSED PRESERVATION OPPORTUNITY:
  THE 3FT RAVENGLASS & ESKDALE RAILWAY .... page 67
5 SUFFOLK ENTERPRISE:
  THE SOUTHWOLD RAILWAY .... page 81
6 REMUNERATIVE RAILWAYS FOR NEW COUNTRIES:
  RANSOMES & RAPIER LTD .... page 99
7 THE OLDEST ELECTRIC RAILWAY IN THE WORLD:
  THE VOLKS ELECTRIC RAILWAY .... page 107
8 THE GOLFERS' TRAMWAY:
  THE RYE & CAMBER RAILWAY .... page 117
9 BIRMINGHAM'S NARROW GAUGE TRAMWAYS .... page 131
10 THE RAILWAY FROM NOWHERE TO NOWHERE:
  THE LEEK & MANIFOLD RAILWAY .... page 151
11 ENGLISH LOCOMOTIVE MANUFACTURING FOR THE WORLD:
  THE HUNSLET ENGINE COMPANY .... page 171
12 THE LAST STEAM-WORKING SYSTEM:
  THE BOWATERS PAPER RAILWAY .... page 179

Published by
LIGHTMOOR PRESS
© Lightmoor Press & Michael Whitehouse 2024
Designed by Jess Taylor

British Library Cataloguing-in-Publication Data.
A catalogue record for this book is available from the British Library
ISBN: 9781915069 36 8

All rights reserved. No part of this publication may be reproduced, stored in a retrieval system or transmitted in any form or by any means, electronic, mechanical, photocopying, recording or otherwise, without the written permission of the publisher.

LIGHTMOOR PRESS
Unit 144B, Harbour Road Trading Estate, Lydney,
Gloucestershire GL15 4EJ
www.lightmoor.co.uk / info@lightmoor.co.uk

Lightmoor Press is an imprint of Black Dwarf Lightmoor Publications Ltd

Printed in Poland
www.lfbookservices.co.uk

The 'Calthrop' Locomotive Manifold Railway. [John Alsop collection]

INTRODUCTION

The earliest railways were crude wooden trackways built to guide wheel-mounted wooden tubs used in extracting ore and coal from mines. Because space in the mine tunnels was limited and, as it was necessary for such tubs to be small enough to be pushed by one man, these trackways were almost all built to a narrow gauge.

With the arrival of the Industrial Revolution, demand for coal and minerals increased to satisfy the needs of new industries. Mines and quarries were developed and horse power introduced as the natural and indeed only means of haulage, apart from manpower. Vast numbers of horses were needed to keep pace with demand and enable the mines to feed fast-growing factories. These horses had to be fed and watered, but the cost of oats and hay was increasing. The advent of the Napoleonic Wars saw to that, with its demand for horses and foodstuffs to feed them.

As we have now painfully relearned following the covid pandemic, significant disruption to the established world order changes the status quo. This results in increased cost of labour and materials and so prompts development of inventions to do things differently, either to seek to reduce cost or speed delivery. On top of all this, the Corn Laws of 1815 ensured that mine and transport companies began to look for different ways of doing things rather than continue to rely on the horse. Money began to flow to encourage entrepreneurs such as William Hedley, Timothy Hackworth, George Stephenson, Matthew Murray, John Blenkinsop and Richard Trevithick to build iron wagonways and develop steam engines to supplant horses.

So it was that at the beginning of the Industrial Revolution, it became possible to build railways with iron tracks and wheels, which reduced the friction involved in moving wagons which, initially, enabled horses to power longer wagon trains. Railways then began to develop to connect mines to transshipment points on waterways and the sea. An early, and maybe the first, such railway, was the Lake Lock Rail Road, a three mile long horse-drawn narrow gauge railway in West Yorkshire.

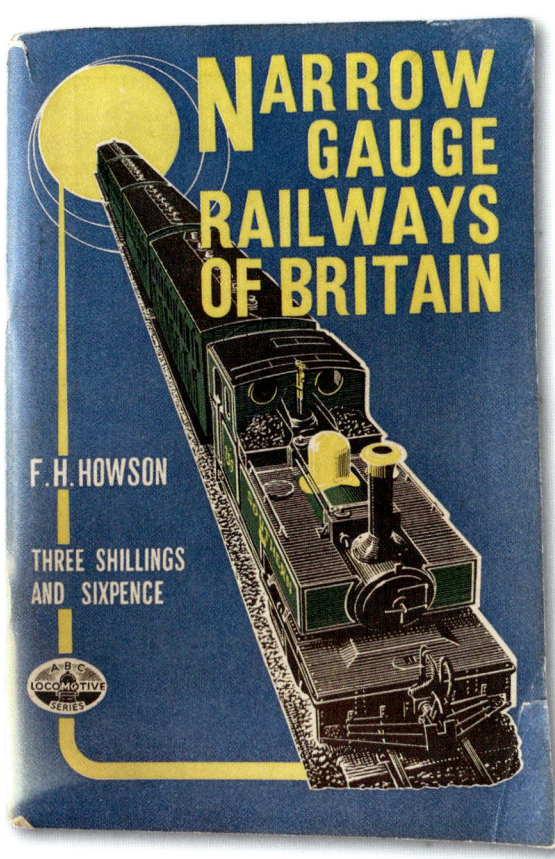

This delightful and informative little booklet was produced in 1948 by Ian Allan and described some twenty narrow gauge and miniature railways around Britain. Howson begins his introduction thus: 'There are fewer narrow gauge railways operating in Britain today than there were fifty years ago. Several have been absorbed by the great Railway Companies, and their tracks have been widened to standard gauge, whilst others have had to close because they could not compete with motor bus services. Their story, however, is most interesting, and some …are novel and fascinating, as the reader will discover in this book.'

During this period, the development of the stationary steam engine was proceeding to the point where early steam railway locomotives were being proposed. In 1804, Richard Trevithick demonstrated the first locomotive railway in the world: the four foot Penydarren Tramway, although this was a short-lived experiment. In 1812, the 4ft 1 inch gauge Middleton Railway in Leeds became the first in the world to make commercial use of steam locomotives.

No one really thought of these early railways being specifically narrow gauge. They were simply constructed to a track gauge which was locally suitable, largely on account of the mine tubs or wagons already having set the width of the distance between the rails. This led to railways being built to multiple different gauges. Perhaps, this did not matter until they began to grow in size and length and connect with each other to begin to form national systems. This came to ahead when systems of 7ft ('broad gauge') and 4ft 8 $^{1}/_{2}$ inches ('standard gauge') were developed.

Following the initial flurry of railway construction in Britain in the mid-19th century, some legislation was then deemed necessary to begin to regulate their development and also encourage promotion of railways in more rural communities. This produced three main Acts of Parliament in the 19th century which set the regime for railways and also tramways in Britain.

The first, the Gauge Act of 1848 arose to sort out emerging transshipment problems between systems of the two different core gauge systems.

A break of gauge between different railways, with the resulting additional costs of transhipping goods, began to be seen as an unnecessary and undesirable extra operating expense. This largely arose because a network of standard gauge lines had developed to cover the majority of Britain where promoting shareholders could easily see, or be enticed to see, a quick return on investment. Whilst Isambard Kingdom Brunel had developed a network of broad gauge 7ft lines in the south and west of England for the Great Western Railway, this legislation

The Collier. The first recorded painting of a steam locomotive, a watercolour by George Walker of the *Salamanca*. This was the first commercially successful steam locomotive and built for the 4ft 1 inch narrow gauge edge-railed Middleton Railway by Matthew Murray of Holbeck (on premises near to the famous Hunslet Engine Company). This locomotive was also the first to have two cylinders. She took her name from the Duke of Wellington's victory at the battle of *Salamanca*, fought in the same year. Four similar locomotives were built for the railway and were to have a life of up to twenty years' service, although *Salamanca* was destroyed after only six years when her boiler exploded; apparently, the driver had tampered with the boiler safety valves

A 'horse road train' bringing down the stone from Portland quarry to the railway and cableway connecting to Castletown for onward transport by sea barges around 1905. This 4ft 6 inch Merchant's Railway was built for the local stone industry on the Isle of Portland in Dorset in 1826, formed as a joint share company by seventeen quarry agents. The railway and its associated cable incline alleviated the previous horse drawn cart operations which were deemed cruel, especially when hauling stone down the steep escarpment from the quarries to the harbour, particularly for those horses who acted as brakes by being tethered to the rear of the stone carts. An 1804 account of this method described how horses squatted down on their haunches and suffered themselves to be dragged for many yards, struggling with all their strength against the weight that forces them downwards. As we can see in the picture, it took around eight horses to pull a single stone cart along the level on a roadway. [NEIL PARKHOUSE COLLECTION]

Castletown Quay on the Merchant's Railway on the Isle of Portland showing the wagon loads of granite brought down to the harbour by horse tramways. The stone was used to build many of England's most famous buildings, including the Tower of London, St. Paul's Cathedral and Buckingham Palace. [Neil Parkhouse collection]

forced him to give up his dream and all his broad gauge railways were converted to standard gauge by the end of the century. Ireland was treated as a special case and developed a main line system of 5ft 3 inch gauge and feeder 3ft narrow gauge railways. This all led to railways of less than standard gauge being called 'narrow gauge'.

Captain Tyler became Chief Inspector of Railways in 1871. He was renouned for his physical energy in making several railway inspections in a single day, either to see if they were safe for public use or to enquire into the cause of accidents. He can probably be given much of the credit for bringing the potential of narrow gauge railways to the attention of the public. In 1863, he inspected and passed the Festiniog Railway to carry passengers on its nominal two foot gauge line from 1865 and then enthusiastically read a paper on the concept before the Institution of Civil Engineers. A narrow gauge passenger train was regarded as a novel concept to visualise because, up until then, the Railway Regulation (Gauge) Act of 1846 declared all passenger railways of less than the 'standard gauge' of 4ft 8 $\frac{1}{2}$ inches to be illegal. The Festiniog had escaped this restriction because its construction for slate traffic predated this legislation.

Tyler suggested the Gauge Act be repealed: *'There can be no question, that a system of branch lines, costing two-thirds of the branches now ordinarily constructed, and worked and maintained at three-fourths of the expense of those branches, would be of decided benefit to Great Britain and Ireland, and would be most valuable in India and in the colonies; in fact wherever there are people to travel, produce to be transported, or resources to be developed, where it would not be commercially profitable to incur the expense, in the first instance, of a first-class railway.'*

Whilst Tyler was undoubtedly correct, it would prove to be overseas, rather than in England, where promoters and engineers would take up the narrow gauge cause seriously and develop networks. In the British colonies, lines of between 3ft 6 inch, metre or 2ft 6 inches/2ft became prevalent in opening up the interior of the Empire countries for trade. As we have already seen in our companion *French Narrow Gauge Album*, the system for constructing economic railways in France was well thought out with a national enabling system for Economique railways, resulting in huge network of metre gauge lines covering nearly all the country.

However, the concept of a narrow gauge railway now began to be considered more seriously and systematically in Britain following developments in the slate quarries of Wales, albeit piecemeal with individual and separate railways being constructed, as opposed to networks.

The success of the Ffestiniog Railway in Wales triggered a boom in the construction of narrow gauge railways, not just in Britain but around the world. It could be said that the centre of narrow gauge construction was initially in North Wales. The mountains there held large quantities of slate and their narrow valleys and steep hillsides meant that the smaller narrow gauge railways were cost-effective.

Outside Wales, other industries started to use narrow gauge railways to move freight, notably ironstone, limestone, china clay, brick clay and metals. The first public narrow gauge steam railway in England was the East Cornwall Mineral Railway, established in 1872 by its own Act of Parliament and built to 3ft 6 inch gauge to carry mineral traffic. Many common carrier lines were built to connect smaller towns and rural areas to standard gauge railways at a lower cost. The 1880s were the high point of British narrow gauge railways as traffic on many of these lines reached its peak volume and new lines were built across the country. Most of these railways were constructed pursuant to their own Acts of Parliament and so were able to specify the gauge which suited them, so circumnavigating the Gauge Acts

ABOVE: By the middle of the 19th century, steam locomotives were beginning to be developed for use on industrial railways, with the first locomotives appearing around 1860. On many internal systems, such as quarries, the expense of a conventional tank locomotive could not be justified, particularly where the track was of a poor standard and rails of very light section. Such operations continued to rely on horse or manpower to move their wagons, but there was a demand for a suitable cheap light locomotive. Several engineering firms were already building plant such as pumps, cranes, winches and stationary steam engines. So it was relatively easy to progress to build a simple vertical boilered steam locomotive using many existing drawings, patterns and common parts. Whilst De Winton of Caernarfon were probably the most well-known producers of such designs, William Balmforth, trading from Peel Ings Foundry at Rodley, near Leeds, built a few three foot gauge vertical boilered locomotives to an unusual design, incorporating outside frames, outside sloping cylinders and round section connecting rods with marine big ends. One of his designs is seen here at Crooklands in Dalton in Furness with the crew and other workmen gathered round the locomotive gazing at the photographer, who must also have seemed to them as also being something completely novel. [JOHN ALSOP COLLECTION]

LEFT: Line drawing of American built Baldwin 4-6-0T, designed for a limited life transporting supplies and munitions to the World War One front line behind the trenches. Several locomotives of this type were sold cheaply by the War Office after hostilities ceased and examples were bought by the Snailbeach, Welsh Highland and Ashover railways. This drawing depicts Ashover Light Railway No.3.

RIGHT: Captain Sir Henry Whatley Tyler (7th March 1827 – 30th January 1908). He was a strong protagonist of narrow gauge railways and a pioneering British engineer and politician. Tyler contributed to the Great Exhibition of 1851 and his collections helped found the Science Museum in South Kensington. Tyler was appointed an Inspecting Officer for railways in 1853 – a function which is normally carried out by Royal Engineers officers – holding the position for 24 years.

Southwold Railway's second No. 1 *Southwold*, a 2-4-2T, seen at Halesworth in 1929 being dismantled after the railway's closure. A railway built by local entrepeneurs as the town of Southwold was ignored by the Great Eastern Railway which preferred its connection to the port of Lowestoft. Although this three foot narrow gauge railway was initially successful, it was always overshadowed by the GER and Lowestoft, so attempts to have it taken over and regauged were thwarted despite plans to enlarge and improve the harbour at Southwold. The motor bus finally finished off all traffic expectations and the Second World War sealed the railway's fate. [DAVE WALDREN COLLECTION]

and making Captain Tyler's suggestion of repeal unnecessary.

The second piece of legislation, the Tramways Act, 1870, extended this regulation to address construction of tramways in urban environments and establish a standard protocol to develop these, rather than leave such development entirely to the market and promoters. We will meet this in the chapter on Birmingham's tramways.

The third significant piece of legislation was the Light Railways Act, 1896. This was enabling legislation which encouraged Commissioners to approve specific schemes, including the gauge of each railway. It was designed to assist and simplify the construction and operation of railways at a lower cost. The concept was to enable those communities which had been left out of the railway mania construction in the 19th century, to have some chance of developing their own railways to connect to the standard gauge main line network at a reasonable cost and, potentially, with government grant support.

But, by and large, this legislation came along too late to make a significant difference and most of these light railways, whilst initially reasonably successful, failed in the medium to long term, simply because following the next major war between 1914-18, further significant change occurred in transport with the development of road motor transport and yet further increases in the cost of labour and materials.

But, for the railway enthusiast, this was largely to prove good news, as those lines which were built developed their own idiosyncratic character and were operated by a wide range of different and largely attractive steam locomotives and rolling stock. This endured them to history if not commerce. Hence this book.

In addition to Captain Tyler, there were other engineers who advocated the adoption of narrow gauge railways. Obviously, their promotion of the cause was in self interest for business, but they had justification in promoting their cause. In this book we will consider John Barraclough Fell and Richard Rapier. In a future volume on Welsh Narrow Gauge Railways, we will consider James Spooner.

As we will see in more detail in the first three essays in this book, Fell was an ardent promoter of the narrow gauge. In his address to the Liverpool Engineering Society on 11th September, 1878, he referred to both his and Rapier's approaches. Fell patented systems for light weight construction on wooden trestles to avoid heavy engineering costs over undulating country. Rapier promoted minimum-cost mechanical elements and lightweight track, and in general represented a more economic scheme.

But the number of public common carrier narrow gauge light railways in England could be counted on the fingers of both hands. By the time the Light Railways Act of 1896 was enacted, England had largely built a very comprehensive main line railway system and few areas were remote from some form of railway communication. In this comparatively small island there were not the vast, untouched areas of country that there were overseas, even after those countries' main line railways had been developed. So the most that could be hoped for was probably the promotion of scattered individual railways penetrating untouched enclaves of territory.

A charming picture showing the grass overgrown rope worked incline on the Clay Cross quarry system with a series of wooden wagons anchored to the rope cable. This connected with the Ashover Light Railway, the last light railway to be built in England which was worked by ex-War Office American Baldwin Locomotive Co. 4-6-0Ts. [JOHN ALSOP COLLECTION]

Two of the Southam Cement Works Peckett 0-4-0STs, *Mesozoic* and *Jurassic*. Southams had five of these delightful locomotives built between 1903-13. The others were named *Neozoic*, *Liassic* and *Triassic*. *Mesozoic* still exists in dismantled state at Bromyard, *Liassic* is at the Statfold Barn Railway, *Triassic* is at the Bala Lake Railway, *Jurassic* is on the Lincolnshire Coast Railway at Skegness, *Triassic* and *Neozoic* have been scrapped. [H.C. CASSERLEY, COURTESY DAVE WALDREN COLLECTION]

This legislation established a simplified procedure for obtaining authorisation, so that individual Acts of Parliament were no longer necessary. Instead, promoters applied to the Light Railway Commissioners for a Light Railway Order which was either granted or not. The Commissioners' Order was then passed to the Board of Trade for final examination and approval.

Local authorities were encouraged to promote, finance and even work light railways on their own account or in collaboration with private interests. Financing by a local authority was further encouraged for, if funds were so advanced, the company could, under certain conditions, obtain a loan from the Treasury of up to a quarter of the construction cost. Furthermore, the Treasury was also empowered to make a free grant of up to half the cost if either the Board of Trade or the Board of Agriculture certified that a railway was necessary for the development of a particular area, provided that all parties cooperated in the provision of land and amenities and the grant did not exceed £1 million.

Colonel Holman F. Stevens excelled in manipulating these provisions as we will see in the Torrington & Marland Railway essay. Stephens became a well-known operator of railways which would otherwise have been lost causes; he centralised management overheads and used largely second hand equipment to minimise cost and so kept several railways going which might otherwise have expired. The Snailbeach Railway (which we will meet in Volume 2) is also a good example.

All this still left private enterprise in control, so the factor eventually governing whether a light railway was built or not was whether the promoters believed they would receive a commercial return. Most of the financial powers given to the public sector under this legislation were actually taken up by the construction of urban tramways.

A number of genuine, independent light railways were built under the Act, but by the outbreak of the First World War there were ominous warnings that road transport might provide a better bet. This war largely stopped any further significant advancement and by the time it ended, any chance of achieving a useful light railway network under British conditions had been lost for ever. Public narrow gauge lines in Britain then began to struggle financially.

The 1920s saw a brief resurgence of the narrow gauge as surplus equipment from the War Department became available. Several industrial railways were built using second-hand War Office equipment. Other lines were able to replace ageing locomotives relatively cheaply and continue to operate on shoestring budgets. The last narrow gauge commercial carrier in Britain was the Ashover Light Railway, which opened in 1925 using surplus war equipment. This was the epitome of cheaply-constructed light railways. The use of narrow gauge railways in industry, however, continued to flourish. Many small railways

J.B. Earle, one of the two Kitson 2-6-4Ts built for the Leek & Manifold Light Railway in Derbyshire to the direction of E.R. Calthrop, engineer to the railway, who sought to apply his Indian colonial principles to constructing and equipping light railways to provide the most effective use, but at the lowest cost. Kitson were simply instructed to follow the colonial design Calthrop had devised for the Indian Barsi Light Railway and happily obliged, right down to the last detail, including the enormous front headlight. The photograph shows an early test train formed of *J.B. Earle* and two of the primrose painted wide bodied balcony carriages running along the brand new railway as evidenced by the clean and tidy stone embankments and the new wooden fencing. [E. HARRISON, PETER JOHNSON COLLECTION]

Introduction

The flame that never dies. This site is now marked by an open space sculpture marking the days of the industrial revolution. Tommy is seen here hauling an 18 inch gauge wagon at the Goldendale Iron Company on 3rd March, 1957. This pig iron works at Tunstall near Stoke on Trent was opened by the Williamson Brothers in 1848 and closed in the 1960s. This is the most recent dated photograph accompanying this introduction, despite showing a horse drawn wagon loaded with timber. It is perhaps salutary to conclude this section with the following quotation found on the internet just before publication:

'Well after hours of searching, and asking a few locals via social media, we have discovered that it was once Goldendale Iron Works. Today has been really interesting and touching in a number of ways really, but discovering the past of this area has been one of the things on this project that has put a lump in my throat. There is not a lot of this left now, just the car park, flooded pits and some 1960s pre fab buildings that are collapsing. The site is vast and it speaks volumes of Stoke on Trent's industrial past. The location is perfect for the industrial age, with canal links via the mile long Harecastle tunnel and the railway tracks dividing the site.

Up until the 1960s closures of this plant and many others like it, or the mines, or the pot banks, would have been where the inhabitants of Stoke on Trent would work. Deprivation brought about by the closure of plants such as these is an ongoing characteristic of Stoke, it has never really recovered in the way other centres of industry did such as Manchester's mills or Liverpool's ports. Stoke's pot banks lay in ruins.

You can look at stats, telling us how many households are claiming benefits. You can look at the council cut backs in spending in the name of austerity. But the reality of the situation smacks you in the face when you see industry crumble away and new Eco call centre spaces go unused.'

A row of wooden 4-wheeled tippler wagons, led by four ending tipping wagons, on the Furzebrook Railway, photographed on 20th January 1956. This railway had over a hundred wooden wagons for the movement of china clay. The end tippers were built by J. Newbery & Sons of Wareham as late as between 1948-1954 and the remainder in the railway's own carpenters. The railway's wagons were left as plain unpainted timber, but with ironwork picked out in black. Before 1939, the company imported its wood from Estonia which consisted of red or white deal in its tenth year of growth. This wood was formed of complete trees, cut down and 'squared off' so that the result was inherently much stronger than a sawn plank. The wagon frames were constructed from seasoned local oak from Hampshire or Dorset which was planed and hand finished. [H.C. CASSERLEY, DAVE WALDREN COLLECTION]

were built to serve sand and gravel pits, cement works and the peat and timber extraction industries.

The continued development of road transport and the economic crisis of the 1930s saw a slow decline in the use of narrow gauge railways across the country. The Second World War pushed many struggling enterprises into bankruptcy as labour and materials were diverted to the war effort. During and immediately after the war, the majority of the remaining lines closed.

But this is not the whole story. As inventors of the steam engine and early builders of railways, British companies gained experience which they put to good use, both in generating profits for themselves, but also in developing Britain's place in the world. Early contractors gained the advantage and began to build railways all over Europe and then beyond, particularly in the Empire, but also beyond that, as far away as South America and China. Locomotive and rolling stock manufacturers sprang up in England (and also Scotland) to provide trains and equipment for these railways and this became a huge growth market, far beyond servicing the few small English narrow gauge railways. And far more successful, both in relation to the developments but also in the design, power and operation of their locomotives. The scale and size of these overseas narrow gauge railways far exceeded anything ever built in England: railways hundreds of miles long, opening up continents, scaling mountain ranges and enabling colonisation of the Empire.

The English-designed and built narrow gauge locomotives were diverse and larger too, ranging from the ubiquitous 0-6-0T right up to multiple-wheeled articulated locomotives. So we will consider some of these as well, especially where their entrepreneurs built and developed both English narrow gauge railways and then went on to seek business within the Empire with locomotives and carriages built in Leeds, Birmingham, Manchester and Suffolk: famous names such as Beyer Peacock, Hunslet, Manning, Wardle, Metropolitan Railway Carriage & Wagon and Ransomes & Rapier. These lines were really an extension of the concept of English narrow gauge railway design, just operated in foreign countries, as all the design work, manufacturing and testing was carried out in our country.

Indeed, the very last narrow gauge steam locomotives to be built in England were destined for South Africa and Indonesia and were standard designs developed by the manufacturing companies for sale to anyone. Our story would be incomplete without considering both these and the War Office surplus equipment, built in the United States for front line use in World War One in Europe and then finding a use in keeping some of our own English narrow gauge lines alive and even creating new ones.

So turn the pages to learn more about various individual projects and their varied success and enjoy the pictures. As enthusiasts of railways, their history and development we are lucky to have had this kaleidoscope of narrow gauge railways, even if most are no longer with us.

Michael Whitehouse
Worcestershire, 2024

1
MINIMUM GAUGE

*'There seems little doubt but that small locomotives can be
profitably substituted for horses in many situations.'*
[*The Locomotive Magazine*, 1866]

Arthur Heywood promoted 15 inches as the minimum gauge and the most economical form of transport for country estates and institutions. He built a railway on his estate for family fun and serious demonstration for its potential with sharp curves, inclines and even a viaduct. As he had connections, he courted the military but, apart from the Duke of Westminster who took him up on a proposition to build a 15 inch gauge estate railway at Eaton Hall in Cheshire, his efforts fell on stony ground. Had he enlarged his minimum gauge to 18 inches however, he might have had more luck, for this gauge saw phenomenal use at several military sites which completely overshadow the 'two foot and more' lines we are all used to hearing about.

In 18 inch gauge, there were three takers: railway workshops, the military and industrial & estate users. All these lines were functional, rather than recreational with locomotives specifically designed for them and all in completely different styles.

The earliest 18 inch gauge railway was laid down at Crewe works in 1862 under the direction of the London & North Western Railway's Chief Mechanical Engineer, John Ramsbottom. This system did not have a fully integrated set of lines as some were simply laid down to serve a particular area of the works and so had no need of connections. The introduction of steam locomotives on this workshop railway predated the Festiniog Railway by a year, although it was still not the world's first use of steam on the narrow gauge.

In 1887, the Lancashire & Yorkshire Railway also adopted an 18 inch gauge system at its Horwich works and Beyer, Peacock did likewise at its Gorton factory, with one delightful locomotive called *Dot*.

Crewe Works was linked with the station by a suspension bridge, built in 1878, and 18 inch gauge tracks were even laid on this bridge enabling parts, stores and other components to be taken from the works to the station quickly, so as to enable their transportation wherever they were required on the L&NWR system in times of need. [PETER JOHNSON COLLECTION]

Tiny and a cast iron wagon stand in the tender shop on the Crewe works 18 inch gauge system. *Tiny* entered service in May, 1862 and so predated the Festiniog Railway George England locomotives by a year. In this picture she is in fully lined L&NWR livery and kept in good order. [R.P. Richards]

After the Crewe system, the next 18 inch gauge users were the military who established 18 inch gauge service lines at Chatham and Woolwich in the late 1860s and early 1870s and, in 1915, at Deptford for the Royal Army Service Corps. On these lines, the equipment was larger than at Crewe as the loading gauge was more generous and the curvature less severe and also there were passenger use requirements. The Woolwich system extended to over a hundred miles, greater than any other narrow gauge railway in Britain.

Later in the 19th century and early 20th, some industrial users and estates also adopted 18 inch gauge, two notable lines being at John Knowles Ltd of Woodville in Leicestershire and the Sand Hutton Light Railway in the early 1920s, the latter being constructed pursuant to the Light Railways Act. The John Knowles system adopted 18 inch gauge on account of restricted space at the mine workings and, through the design of the two locomotives they ordered from Hunslet, they connected the 18 inch gauge story to both the military and Sand Hutton. But we should begin at the beginning.

At Crewe, Ramsbottom quickly recognised the need to increase efficiency and speed of delivery within the works to facilitate the movement of materials, equipment and components and replace much manpower and the use of horses and carts. But the works had restricted spaces and it was out of the question to develop a standard gauge integrated system, so a number of sections of 18 inch gauge were installed instead, still retaining some hand shunting in local areas. To work these lines, Ramsbottom arranged for the design of some very distinctive steam locomotives which gave good service for the life of the railway. The first locomotive was appropriately named *Tiny* and entered service in May, 1862. It was used in the Old Works.

The Old Works was linked with the station at Crewe by a suspension bridge, built in 1878, and 18 inch gauge tracks were even laid on this bridge enabling parts, stores and other

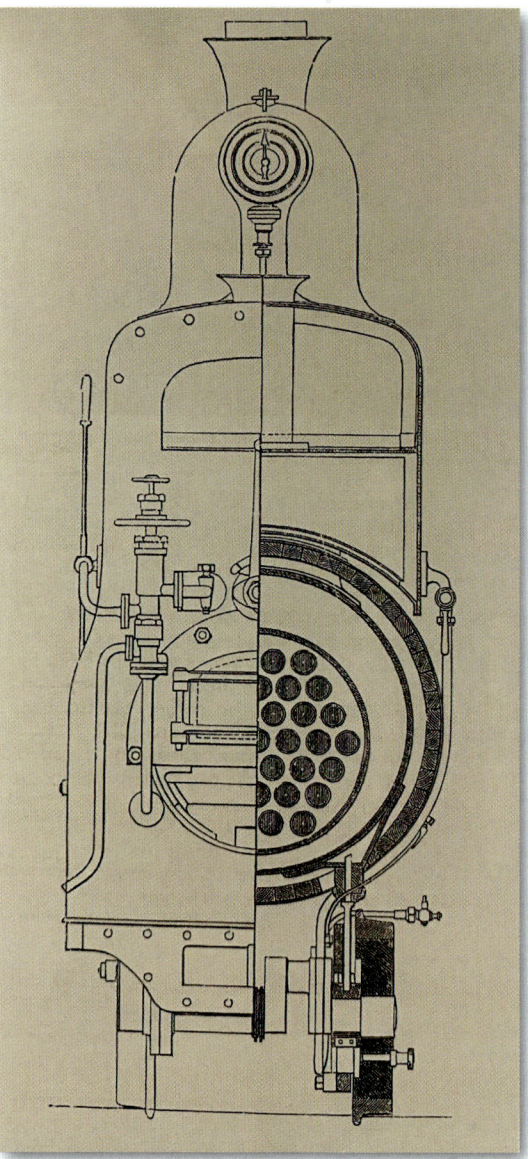

A drawing of *Tiny* published in the *Engineering* magazine on 19th January 1866 which emphasises her diminutive size and described it as having 'inside cylinders 4 $\frac{1}{4}$ inch diameter and 6 inch stroke, and the wheels are 15 $\frac{1}{4}$ inch in diameter and placed 3 inches apart from centre to centre. The boiler, which is 4ft 6 in long between end plates, and 2ft diameter outside is made of two plates "butt jointed". It contains a flue or firebox 2ft 5 $\frac{5}{8}$ inches long and 1ft 5 $\frac{1}{4}$ inches diameter inside, the€ firebox being forged solid out of one plate and flanged over at the end for attachment to the end plate of the boiler…The engine is carried upon four India rubber spring. Both the tank and coal box are situated above the boiler…The boiler is fed by a pump worked from one of the crossheads, and also by a No. 2 Giffard injector. The engine is 7ft 7 inches long over buffer plates and 2ft 6 inches wide and its total weight in working order is 2 $\frac{1}{2}$ tons. There seems little doubt but that small locomotives of a class resembling [this] can be profitably substituted for horses in many situations'.

components to be taken from the works to the station quickly, so as to enable their transportation wherever they were required on the L&NWR system in times of need. Another locomotive of the same design, *Midge* was used on this trip working which led to the bridge being called the 'Midge bridge'. Access to this bridge was by a steep incline and exit to the platforms through the middle of a signalbox.

The largest sections of the Crewe works narrow gauge system were in the 'steel works', although that area also catered for other construction activities. There was an isolated section of railway in the paint shop, but this was always hand worked. Other sections served the signal shop, new machine shop, erecting shop and deviation shop, the newest area of the works, with track reaching three levels to which wagons were raised by capstans; this section lasted as long as 1967, albeit hand worked.

The design of the steam locomotives for this set of lines was intriguing and unorthodox, but proven in use. They were only three feet wide and, unusually for such a small design, fitted with inside frames and cylinders so as to keep width to a minimum. The water tank was perched on top of the boiler, giving a top heavy appearance, and the chimney and large steam collecting dome on top of that. The firebox was of marine type and cylindrical, contiguous with the boiler. The locomotives were provided with both boiler water feedpumps, as usual in early shunting locomotives, but also No. 2 Giffard injectors; Ramsbottom was the first British main line engineer to use injectors on his locomotives. The total height of these locomotives (to the top of the chimney) was 10ft $\frac{3}{4}$in.

Tiny worked well straight off the drawing board and so others soon followed: *Pet*, *Nipper*, *Topsy* and *Midge*. All locomotives were painted in black but also smartly lined out in standard L&NWR red and grey. Apart from later reducing the height of their chimneys in order to access even more restricted areas of the works, these locomotives were little altered during their lifetime. All were scrapped in 1929, except *Pet* which survives in

A lovely posed photograph of *Midge* with her driver looking at the plate glass camera and standing perfectly still for the time exposure. The photograph was taken in the Old Works Yard and *Midge* is coupled to a locomotive stores 4-wheeled truck. [LNWR Society collection]

'Dignity & Impudence'. A drawing showing *Nipper* as built in 1887, posed alongside single wheeler *Cornwall*.

Nipper, very clean and in good condition, also lined out in L&NWR passenger locomotive livery, most probably photographed before World War One. [NATIONAL RAILWAY MUSEUM]

In October, 1873 F.W. Webb succeeded Ramsbottom and, four years later, produced his own design of 18 inch gauge locomotives for Crewe Works with two locomotives: *Billy* and *Dickie*, both seen here in official L&NWR photographs painted in photographic works grey livery and fully lined out, clearly showing their July 1875 and May 1876 build dates (respectively) on the L&NWR standard design of nameplate. They are both standing on an 18 inch gauge crossover with the Old Works yard's standard gauge lines. These locomotives were actually designed by William Rylance, a senior chargehand entrusted with special projects who signed his job sheets as 'Wm. Rylance & Co'. This gave rise to the mistaken impression that an outside contractor of this name actually built these two locomotives which underlines the care needed in latter day research once all relevant people have moved on. *Billy* was named after Rylance. *Engineering* magazine commented once again on the novel design: *'The boilers are cylindrical, and each is traversed by a hexagonal flue strengthened by small cross tubes, which present very efficient heating surface. From the flue three chimneys pass up through the steam dome, each chimney being provided with a blast nozzle.'* *Billy* was originally built with a Brotherhood 3-cylinder engine, but is seen in this picture rebuilt with outside cylinders like *Dickie*.

[LNWR Society collection]

In May, 1888, *Dickie* was used in haulage trials on a mile long stretch of track constructed on the tow path of the Middlewich branch of the Ellesmere & Chester Canal, with the locomotive hauling up to eight boats and achieving a speed of 7mph. F.W. Webb himself is on the left. [LNWR SOCIETY COLLECTION]

the national collection. Later, in the 1870s, under F.W. Webb's Superintendency, two more locomotives of different design and operable from either end were built: *Billy* and *Dickie*, the first named after a senior chargehand. In May, 1888, *Dickie* was used in haulage trials on a mile long stretch of track constructed on the tow path of the Middlewich branch of the Ellesmere & Chester canal with the locomotive hauling up to eight boats and achieving a speed of 7mph. *Dickie* was also withdrawn in 1929, but *Billy* survived until 1931 and was replaced by diesel traction, a 4-wheeled locomotive built by Hudswell, Clarke and named *Crewe*, later transferred to Horwich.

In 1887, the Lancashire & Yorkshire engineer, John Aspinall, introduced a similar 18 inch gauge system at the Horwich works. This system, initially 2 ³/₄ miles, but later extended to 7 miles, lasted until the 1960s and at least one of its locomotives, *Wren*, lived long enough to receive BR fully-lined mixed traffic livery before being withdrawn for preservation in the national collection in 1962. Aspinall did not produce the locomotives to be used at Horwich, choosing instead to order three from Beyer, Peacock named *Robin*, *Wren* and *Dot*. Beyer, Peacock also built one to the same design for its own internal works system, also called *Dot* which, perhaps, looked more ornate as it was only equipped with a well tank (and not an additional saddle tank) which enhanced its ornate shapely lines. Fortunately, the Beyer, Peacock *Dot* has also been preserved (at the Narrow Gauge Railway Museum in Tywyn). A further two almost identical locomotives were built for Horwich in 1891: *Wasp* and *Fly*, but these were built at Horwich, followed by another two in 1899: *Mouse* and *Midget* and a final class member, *Bee*, in 1901. Operating experience required more water and coal than originally provided for, so small tenders and water tanks over the boiler were later added.

As an introduction to considering the military 18 inch gauge railways and also generally in the development of narrow gauge railways designed to minimise construction cost, we must first consider the work of John Barraclough Fell as he was to have quite an involvement with some of the other railways included in this book, as well as some innovations overseas. Fell exercised a great deal of innovative effort and displayed much competence, all of which produced fascinating outcomes which also worked as intended. But it is also probably fair to say that Fell 'over thought' the needs of cheaply constructed light railways and, as we will see in succeeding chapters, was obliged to modify some of his ideas in practice.

Fell originated from the English Lake District and introduced steam boats on Windermere, which brought him into professional contract with the famous railway builders of the mid 19th century: Joseph Locke and Thomas Brassey. By the early 1860s, Fell had secured Brassey's confidence and together they set to work designing and building the amazing Mont Cenis railway, running through a pass in the alps which had been used since antiquity. Pending completion of a tunnel through the alps, these engineers devised a railway to climb over the mountains and introduced operations just before the American Mount Washington cog railroad, which claims the title of the first mountain rack railway. How is all this relevant to the development of the English narrow gauge railway? Read on and also consider the essays on the Pentewan and

Crewe was the first diesel locomotive to work on the London Midland & Scottish Railway. It was built by Hudswell Clarke & Co. Ltd in 1930 for the Crewe Works 18 inch gauge system and powered by a 20hp 3-cylinder McLaren Benz diesel engine which drove the 1ft 3 inch diameter wheels by means of a jackshaft and a connecting rod. In 1932, when the Crewe system was abandoned, it was transferred to Horwich.
[W. LESLIE GOOD, MICHAEL WHITEHOUSE COLLECTION]

Torrington & Marland railways which follow.

Fell applied himself to the problem of enabling steam trains to climb over mountains. With Thomas Brassey's approval, Fell exploited the concept of a third rail with horizontally-mounted driving wheels on the locomotives and rolling stock spring loaded onto this centre rail, so as to provide a higher tractive effort than ordinary adhesive weight. This worked well and the Mont Cenis railway served its purpose until the tunnel was built.

On 23rd September, 1870, Fell then read a paper before the British Association at Liverpool on centre rail railways and also the advantages of narrow gauge railways. He reported:

'Plans have been laid before the War Office for accelerating military transport in foreign countries and before the Governor-general of India for the construction of cheap branches. The gauge of these railways may be from 6 inches to 18 inches. They may be of wood or iron and may be worked by either stationary engines or by locomotives. They have the advantage of being economical in both construction and working, they occupy little land...they may be erected with great rapidity and, being portable, may be removed when no longer required.'

Fell, seeking more work, constructed a short monorail to link the Parkhouse Haematite Mine with the Furness Railway near Barrow-in-Furness. But, as the carrying capacity of the monorail was insufficient, it was rebuilt on elevated wooden trestles with two bearing rails at a gauge of 8 inches, and with wagons built having a low centre of gravity and four horizontal guide wheels running on rails placed at a lower level, designed to steady the loads. Fell was satisfied that this worked well and so approached the War Office seeking further business. This was good timing as the Royal Engineers were then considering the best way to construct railways rapidly within a war zone at a rate of several miles a day. The War Office wanted a standard form of railway transport which could be issued to the Royal Engineers and kept ready for use with men trained in its operation. In their minds, they envisaged a standard gauge system for transport to a rail head and then a narrow gauge system of trench railways.

The Royal Engineers visited the Parkhouse 'railway' and quickly formed the view that this sort of enterprise could be quickly built and used over uneven ground. Indeed, they commented that such a concept would have been invaluable in both the Crimea and Abyssinia. So, Fell was commissioned by the War Office to design an experimental portable railway in 18 inch gauge capable of using 1 in 50 gradients for evaluation. The Royal Engineers specified that the railway was to be built on wooden trestles with variable heights according to the lie of the land, which was expected to reduce construction costs by reducing the earthworks necessary. This experimental mile-long railway was built at Aldershot in the first half of 1872, ten years after the Crewe Works system became operational with steam.

As Manning, Wardle already had six locomotives in use at Woolwich and Chatham, the Leeds firm received an order to supply a locomotive for the experimental railway They built a

Pet out of steam inside the works on 7th June 1930. Fortunately, this locomotive survives in the National Collection and can be seen at the National Railway Museum in York, although it was originally displayed at the Narrow Gauge Railway Museum at Tywyn. *Pet* is displayed in as withdrawn condition, painted in plain black. [Dave Waldren collection]

6-coupled tender locomotive with outside frames and cylinders which was named *Ariel*. Its unorthodox feature was that it had vertical rollers which projected downwards from the frames and bore against the sides of the superstructure on which the railways were laid. Each vehicle had four of these rollers which were to prevent the train derailing. Several tests were run with both freight and passengers and *Ariel* succeeded in hauling loads of 25 tons up 1 in 50 grades and running passenger trains at up to 30mph, with the average being 25mph. The train ran as steadily as any standard gauge railway, even when the passenger train reached speeds of 30mph.

The Royal Engineers even took the railway up and relaid it in a different location to see if Fell's claims in that regard were correct. Fell's claims were vindicated, but the Royal Engineers did not proceed with the concept. There were several reasons for this. First, the elevated system rendered it vulnerable to enemy gunfire. Second, the Royal Engineers had discovered that Fell had, by then, gained the contract to rebuild the Pentewan Railway (see next essay) which would run entirely without major earthworks, simply due to the easy lie of the land and so wrote to Fell to ask if he was now abandoning guide wheels for commercial railways. Fell was obliged to concede this point for when a railway simply ran along the ground.

The Royal Engineers also asked Captain Tyler of the Railway

Minimum Gauge | 27

Portrait of *Wren*. Her ashpan has just been emptied and she sits out of steam. Note the three way point into the shed on the right of the picture. [Dave Waldren collection]

Wren shunting tipping wagons at Horwich on 9th August 1953. [H.C. Casserley, Peter Johnson collection]

Robin and *Wasp* stand side by side on the Horwich Works 18 inch gauge locomotive shed. [W. LESLIE GOOD, MICHAEL WHITEHOUSE COLLECTION]

Inspectorate if there would ever be a pool of locomotives easily available which could be requisitioned at short notice to run on such lines. Tyler confirmed that *'light tank engines of the ordinary gauge would always be procurable for military purposes'*. So, Fell's experiment did not get taken up by the military, but it had still proved of use in satisfying them that a minimum gauge was suitable for their needs and so the concept of the 18 inch gauge was firmly cemented in their minds for their depot railways.

But the Military were not quite finished with innovation on the 18 inch gauge yet. Henry Handyside from New Zealand patented a 'Steep Gradient Apparatus' intended solely for front line military use in minimising the amount of earthworks required to build railways. This invention utilised a conventional railway but adapted the locomotive and rolling stock by the fitment of 'gripping apparatus', capable of holding the locomotive on the incline and effectively turning it into a stationary winch to haul wagons up an incline. An additional set of cylinders were added to the locomotive for this function. The locomotive would run up the incline to a suitable point, winch the wagons up to it, they would then be locked onto the track whilst the locomotive ran further up the incline and the process was repeated until the summit was achieved. It must have been fascinating to watch.

This Handyside system was adopted and funded by Fox, Walker & Co. of Bristol and tried out on the steep standard gauge 1 in 14 Hopton Incline in Derbyshire. The results of the trials did not prove convincing for civilian use, as fixed winding engines were preferred (and indeed the Cromford & High Peak Railway proceeded in this way), but could really assist on the front line if gradients of temporary track at 1 in 10 could be achieved. Fox Walker built some rather ungainly steam locomotives for more military trials, but there were several problems and the scheme was not proceeded with, most probably not only on account of the technical problems but because Major Hogg RE, the Inspector-General of Fortification was unconvinced that 18 inch gauge railways were suitable for the front line for safety or unit cost reasons, preferring metre gauge. All this was against the background of the then threat of a conflict with Russia and so preparations might have been a little too hasty. As it happens, this threat receded and with it, interest in getting this system right. There is much more that could be said about all these experiments, but they would fill another book.

Turning next to the military depot railways, these were large users of 18 inch narrow gauge railways. Their stories would also fill a complete book, so we only have space to consider one of these systems, that at The Royal Arsenal at Woolwich.

The importance of the Royal Arsenal Railway cannot be

RIGHT: *Dot*, the Beyer, Peacock 0-4-0WT works shunter, immaculately repainted by the company for presentation to the Narrow Gauge Railway Museum at Tywyn. [BRIAN HILTON, ANDREW NEALE COLLECTION]

BELOW: *Ariel*, built for the experimental Fell patented railway system at Aldershot by Manning, Wardle. The system involved two bearing rails and four horizontal guide wheels which ran on rails placed at a lower level, designed to steady the loads carried. These can clearly be seen in the picture. The locomotive was intriguing and unusual to fit this system and had cylinders set below the level of the axles and the drive offset from the centre of the crankpin. There was a protective handrail all round both the locomotive and tender. [JOHN ALSOP COLLECTION]

underestimated. Until the First World War, the security of the United Kingdom and the British Empire was totally dependent on the Arsenal and the Arsenal was totally dependent on its railway system.

The Woolwich Arsenal Railway began as far back as 1824 with a horse-drawn plateway, opened a standard gauge system in 1849 (worked by the South Eastern Railway) and opened its 18 inch gauge system in 1871 and largely took over the standard gauge duties except for heavy gun haulage. This managed to find its way into virtually every building within the Arsenal. The railway provided for the movement of both goods and passengers within the Royal Arsenal. The 'main line' was operated on an 'Inner Circle' principle divided into six sections linked by telephone. Passenger trains were run every half hour for the workforce and an average of 400 wagons a day passed over it. Around 3,200 passenger miles were worked daily.

The Crimean War had caused a major increase in ammunition production as it was then realised that iron ordnance needed in-house production facilities and the Royal Gun Factory was developed. The South African War of 1899-1902 saw a further upturn in activity followed, of course, by the First World War. Now, the railway was needed more than ever to move material around the depot. So, the period from 1900 to 1916 saw the 18 inch gauge system grow to become the most extensive locomotive-

Culverin, an 0-4-0ST Hudswell, Clarke No. 269 built in 1894, on an empty stock working at Woolwich Arsenal in 1919. She had the distinction of giving her name to a class of locomotives which were very successful and displaced the Manning, Wardles from main line to shop work. By 1889, there were nine of this class working at Woolwich and five more were built in 1915.
[JOHN ALSOP COLLECTION]

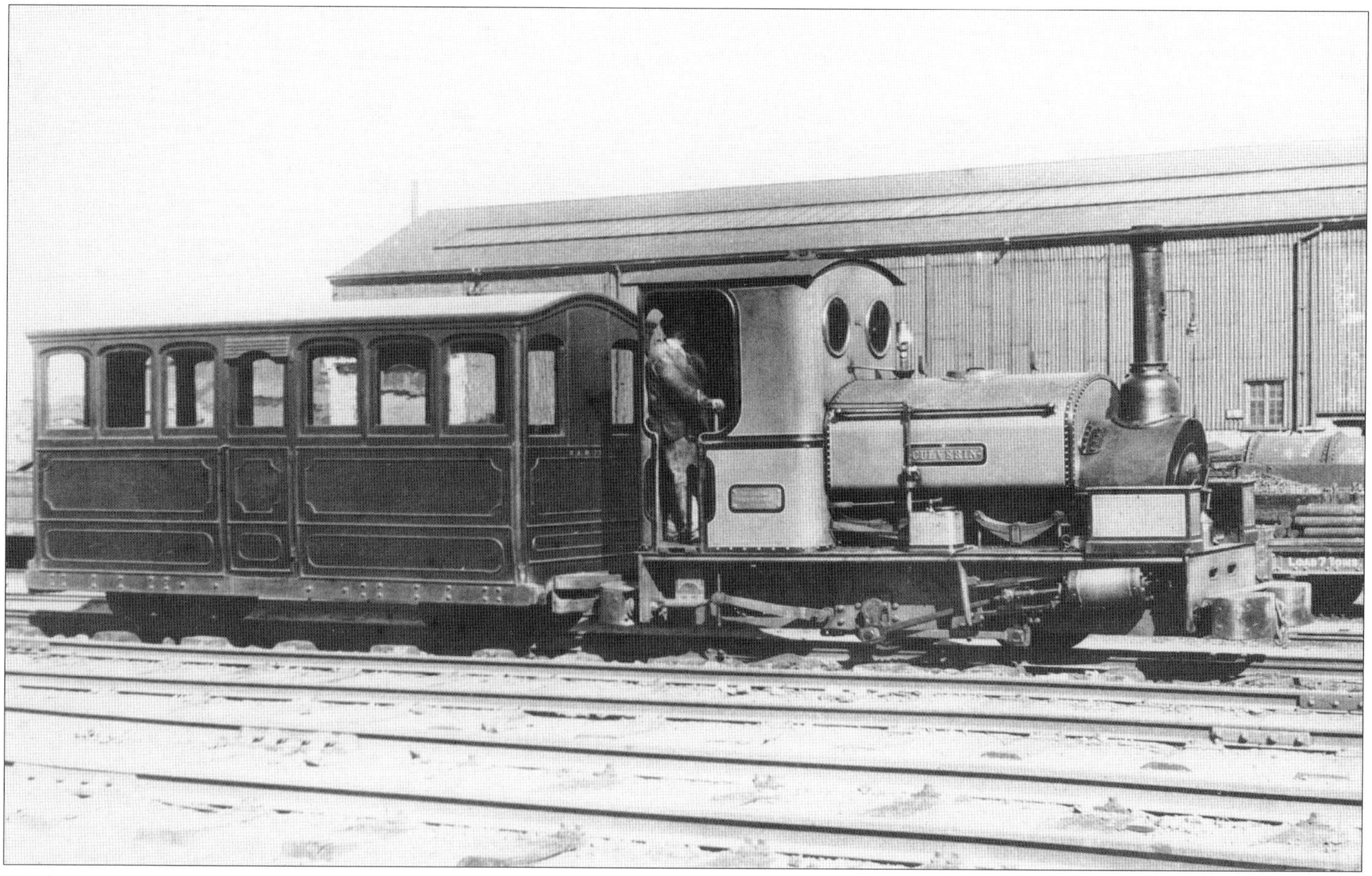

Culverin again, this time with a superintendent's bogie saloon. The locomotive had received a new cab in 1918 but its use was short-lived as the locomotive was scrapped in 1922. She is fitted with a 'Neath' spark arrestor so she could work in the 'Danger Buildings'. These spark arrestors were designed by Mr Neath, the foreman of the locomotive department and fitted in an extended smokebox showing an upwards projecting 'bubble', requiring a shorter chimney. [PETER JOHNSON COLLECTION]

A portrait of *Hannibal*, another of the Hudswell, Clarke 0-4-0STs, No. 281 built in 1885, taken soon after the First World War. Her smokebox and chimney had been replaced since she was built, probably to accommodate the 'Neath' pattern spark arrestor. She was sold by auction in November 1921 and scrapped. [PETER JOHNSON COLLECTION]

Phoenix, built by Kerr, Stuart (No. 809 of 1901) running bunker first on a Woolwich Arsenal passenger train consisting of a two-compartment composite coach and an open 'knifeboard' carriage, the latter (at least) built by Bristol Wagon & Carriage Co. There were at least three designs of bogie carriage in use at this time, namely the original 'knifeboard' open pattern, a closed 1st/2nd Class composite with diagonal body planking and a 'curly roofed' superintendent saloon. [NEIL PARKHOUSE COLLECTION]

Four 'Charlton' Class Avonside 0-4-0Ts inside the locomotive shed with *Enfield* leading, all waiting to be lit up with wood baskets placed alongside. The photograph shows the lining clearly. This class of locomotive was the most modern design to see service on the War Office 18 inch gauge systems and all were built by the Avonside Engine Co. of Bristol between 1915-16 and fitted with side tanks. One, *Woolwich*, has survived into preservation. [DAVE WALDREN COLLECTION]

Avonside *Manchester* on shed with 'D Section' headboard (for the Danger Section ammunition stores). [Dave Waldren collection]

worked narrow gauge railway on the British mainland. This gauge was adopted largely because of the success of the internal Crewe works system and then used at both Woolwich and Chatham. By the 1920s the system had grown to 147 miles with 70 miles of 18 inch gauge, much of it on mixed gauge, with 74 narrow gauge locomotives in operation; quite staggering figures.

This system, along with a similar one operated by the Admiralty at Chatham Dockyard, were important proving grounds for the 'mainstream' outside framed narrow gauge steam locomotive, particularly by the pioneering '6-inch by 8-inch' Manning, Wardle 0-4-0ST locomotives used at both sites. In 1896, internal combustion locomotives were introduced. The first of these, *Lachesis*, was built by R. Hornsby & Sons and was the second internal combustion locomotive built in Britain, and likely the third anywhere in the world. It was certainly the first truly successful internal combustion locomotive.

After the 1918 Armistice, the activities at the Arsenal began to reduce of course and steps were taken to mitigate potential unemployment arising. Milk churns were made for commercial use and, using the experience gained from the railway operations, the works began to build standard gauge steam locomotives for the South Eastern & Chatham Railway. Neither projects were exactly successful and failed to stave off the inevitable run down of the Woolwich railway system between 1919-22 and a mass disposal of its locomotives. In 1935, Hunslet entered the 18 inch gauge field with bogie diesel locomotives, having previously built steam locomotives for The Mechanical Transport Company Army Service Corps Reserve depot at Deptford.

All too soon, the re-armament programme in the 1930s ensured there would be no further run down of the Arsenal's 18 inch gauge system as production then steadily increased up to the Second World War, but the probability of air raids and significant danger of invasion, prompted the decision to disperse stores throughout the United Kingdom, which proved a wise measure as the first enemy attack on the Arsenal on 7th September, 1940 claimed 53 lives and injured a further 247 people.

After the war, a further diversification model was again adopted but, with the Berlin airlift during the Cold War, production was again stepped up. By this time, Ruston & Hornsby had supplied a number of 4-wheeled diesel locomotives and mechanised road transport was also in use. The last of the Avonside 0-4-0T 'Charlton' locomotives, *Woolwich*, (introduced in 1916) was put into store and a new Hunslet double bogie diesel *Carnegie* arrived, fitted with an 88bhp McLaren engine and electric starter motor and became the very last locomotive supplied to the Arsenal. The last flurry of activity was during the Suez Crisis of 1956, then railway operations were run down and, when munitions manufacture ceased in 1967, so did the railway. Both *Woolwich* and *Carnegie* survive and, after a sojourn at Bicton Woodland Railway in

The Hunslet double bogie diesel *Carnegie* on arrival at Woolwich. It was fitted with an 88bhp McLaren engine and electric starter motor, and became the very last locomotive supplied to the Arsenal. Whilst details of this picture have not yet come to light, it seems likely that this is a posed photograph at the handover into service. [STATFOLD NARROW GAUGE MUSEUM TRUST]

John Knowles & Co. (Wooden Box) Ltd's 0-4-0WT 'frame tank' built for the railway by Hunslet in 1898 (Works No. 684) and named *Jack* after the Managing Director's son. The original attractive Midland red colourscheme can just be made out in this undated picture.
[MICHAEL WHITEHOUSE COLLECTION]

Devon, both are now at the Statford Barn Railway and *Carnegie* has been restored and is operable.

Lastly in the 18 inch gauge story, we turn to consider the Hunslet 0-4-0 well tanks, which were called 'frame tanks' by the manufacturer. Eighteen of these locomotives appeared on three systems between 1898 and 1920: industrial, military and a railway enthusiast's estate railway and two even still exist.

John Knowles & Co. (Wooden Box) Ltd owned clay mines and processing plants at Mount Pleasant near Woodville in Leicestershire. When it came to considering the use of steam traction for haulage in 1897, the mine workings had already been equipped with 18 inch gauge railway lines due to restricted clearances which predetermined the gauge of the railway. Three steam locomotives worked on the line during its life: two Hunslet 0-4-0WTs, similar to the Deptford locomotives (and an unsuccessful 0-4-0T built by Bagnall, which we will ignore here!). Hunslet was approached to build the first locomotive, named *Jack* after the Managing Director's son, as Knowles were very satisfied with the standard gauge locomotive they already had to shunt their sidings. Hunslet had never built an 18 inch gauge locomotive before but, in the same city (Leeds), both Manning, Wardle and Hudswell, Clarke were busy making many 18 inch gauge locomotives for the military and it would seem obvious, with hindsight, just to ask one of them to make another locomotive to their standard design. But Hunslet did not let on as, of course, they were quite happy to receive the order. A similar tale recurred when the company wanted a second locomotive (to replace the Bagnall). Somewhat naturally, they approached Hunslet again, who were, of course, happy to oblige and provided a second, slightly larger 'frame tank' but of very similar design in 1920; this was named *Gwen*. What Hunslet did not reveal to John Knowles was that four of exactly the same type were then being disposed of by the Royal Army Service Corps Special Reserve Depot at Deptford. It would undoubtedly have been much cheaper for John Knowles to buy one of those, but it seems they were unaware and so why should Hunslet tell them?

These locomotives were initially turned out in attractive Midland red livery, lined in Naples yellow and with vermillion buffer beams and motion brackets but, of course, they rapidly got very scruffy. They worked efficiently enough until the 1950s, when their run-down state led to the railway's closure in 1958 and its replacement by a rope haulage system. The management were reluctant to see the locomotives scrapped. *Gwen* was sold for £100 to a private buyer in the USA and, whilst she has changed hands, she is still workable. *Jack* was also saved, but nearer to home, initially at the Leeds Industrial Museum at Armley Mills but now to be found at the Statfold Barn Railway.

The last of the military 18 inch gauge military systems to be opened was at the Army Meat Depot at Deptford serving the Royal Army Service Corps. Possibly as some compensation for not being awarded the contract to provide locomotives for Woolwich, Hunslet were commissioned to do so for Deptford during the First World War. They offered a slightly larger version of the design they had already produced for John Knowles. Twelve were delivered in batches and named the 'Waril' Class; essentially very similar to *Jack* but with larger cylinders, a 6 inch longer wheelbase, oil firing and a higher pitched boiler. Once the war was over, inevitably, the depot was run down and the locomotives were surplus to requirements. Four were to find another home.

Major Sir Robert Walker, the fourth Baronet of Sand Hutton in Yorkshire had a lifelong interest in railways and laid out a 15 inch pleasure line on his estate. After the First World War, he resolved to put his railway to more serious use. He incorporated a company and obtained a Light Railway Order for a line serving agricultural and commercial interests on his estate, running for just over five miles between Warthill, connecting with the North Eastern Railway, and Scrayingham. During construction, he realised the need for a 1 in 80 gradient and realised that his model Bassett-Lowke Atlantic locomotive would not be fit for the job. As we have already seen, 18 inch gauge military equipment was now coming up for disposal. This was timely and so Sir Robert bought equipment from Deptford, eventually including four of the Hunslet locomotives (No's 4, 10, 11 and 12), together with some 75 4-wheeled wagons. The locomotives were converted from oil firing to coal and had ornate copper capped chimneys added, retaining their dark green livery. No. 10 was named *Esme* after Sir Robert's second wife. In 1924, this locomotive was fitted with vacuum brake to work with the railway's sole passenger carriage. The locomotives gave good service, their only shortcoming being limited water capacity and lack of a pony truck to give a steadier ride.

The railway ended up only being constructed from Warthill to Bossall and on to Barnby House, with a branch to Claxton, all open for business by the end of 1923. The final half mile to Scrayingham was abandoned due to rising costs and the requirement for a bridge over the River Derwent. Exchange sidings with the NER were built at Warthill.

From the opening in 1924, three return passenger services were run only on Saturdays, to coincide with market days in York but, at least during 1925, these were also run on Wednesdays. Sadly, these only lasted for five years, although passengers may have been carried unofficially in wagons after then. Passenger receipts were hardly high, the best year bringing in £38. The best freight carrying years were between 1926-28, largely derived from agricultural produce, coal and the output of Claxton brickworks until this closed in 1929. In common with so many other narrow gauge lines, competition from lorries and a local bus seriously affected traffic receipts and after Sir Robert died in the following year, the railway was abandoned in 1932. This was all an inevitability. Sir Robert's enthusiasm for railways had carried the day during his lifetime, but the economic depression in the 1930s was the final nail in the coffin. The carriage body survived as a pavilion for the Harton ladies cricket club near Bossall and managed to survive long enough to be acquired for preservation.

THE SAND HUTTON RAILWAY

The Sand Hutton Railway, as a 1ft 6 inch gauge public railway, had a working life almost exactly contemporaneous with the Welsh Highland Railway, and was then about half way through its equally brief and inglorious career. So there was no doubt about the priorities. Enquiries revealed that no train from the Market Weighton direction connected with the Sand Hutton trains, in one case only failing to make the connection by five minutes. Thus I was compelled to go by bicycle.

I made friends with the driver at Warthill. He proved to be no other than Mr Batty himself, the man who, second only to Sir Robert Walker, was the presiding genius of the railway; to my delight he suggested that I might care to travel in the cab with him. It must have been a time of partial drought, for the ordinary watering facilities had run dry, and an unscheduled halt was made at White Syke beck bridge, where the engine tank was replenished by means of a bucket on the end of a rope. The repercussions of this on that sacred timetable may be left to the imagination.

In due course we reached the terminus at Bossall. I was fully informed about the projected extension over the Derwent to Scrayingham, and was shocked and pained to find that anyone connected with the railway could question the desirability of such a consummation, yet Mr Batty was firmly opposed to it, 'for', as he put it, 'ther's nowt at Scrayin'am'. He was of course right; there was 'nowt' at Bossall either for that matter!

The Sand Hutton passenger service was confined to Saturdays, and a curious feature of it was that the running shed being at Sand Hutton depot, and not at one of the terminals, empty stock had to be worked out prior to the departure of the first train and after the final arrival; and not only that, but two empty stock workings over the whole length of the line were demanded by the advertised services.

Even so ardent a devotee of the narrow gauge as myself could find little to love on the Sand Hutton; the 0-4-0WTs were ugly, ungainly, little affairs; the relatively flat landscape deprived it of any interesting earthworks, and the grandiloquently-named White Syke Junction, where the goods only Claxton branch diverged, proved to be no more than an unattended pair of points in the middle of nowhere; no little signal box, no signals, not even a siding. After Sir Robert's death, the line did not survive long. During the first few years of its life, it did its job well; it is said that the bricks for the building of the University of Hull were made at Claxton brick works and passed over the Sand Hutton. In death, as in life, the Sand Hutton passed almost unnoticed and unsung.

Mr Batty, the main driver on the Sand Hutton, stands beside one of the Hunslet 'frame tank' 0-4-0s from the Deptford Army Meat Depot immediately after gauge conversion from 15 inches. The locomotive still has a stovepipe chimney which is the result of having had its Deptford spark arrestor removed, but has not yet been fitted with the stylish copper cap favoured by Sir Herbert Walker. [JOHN ALSOP COLLECTION]

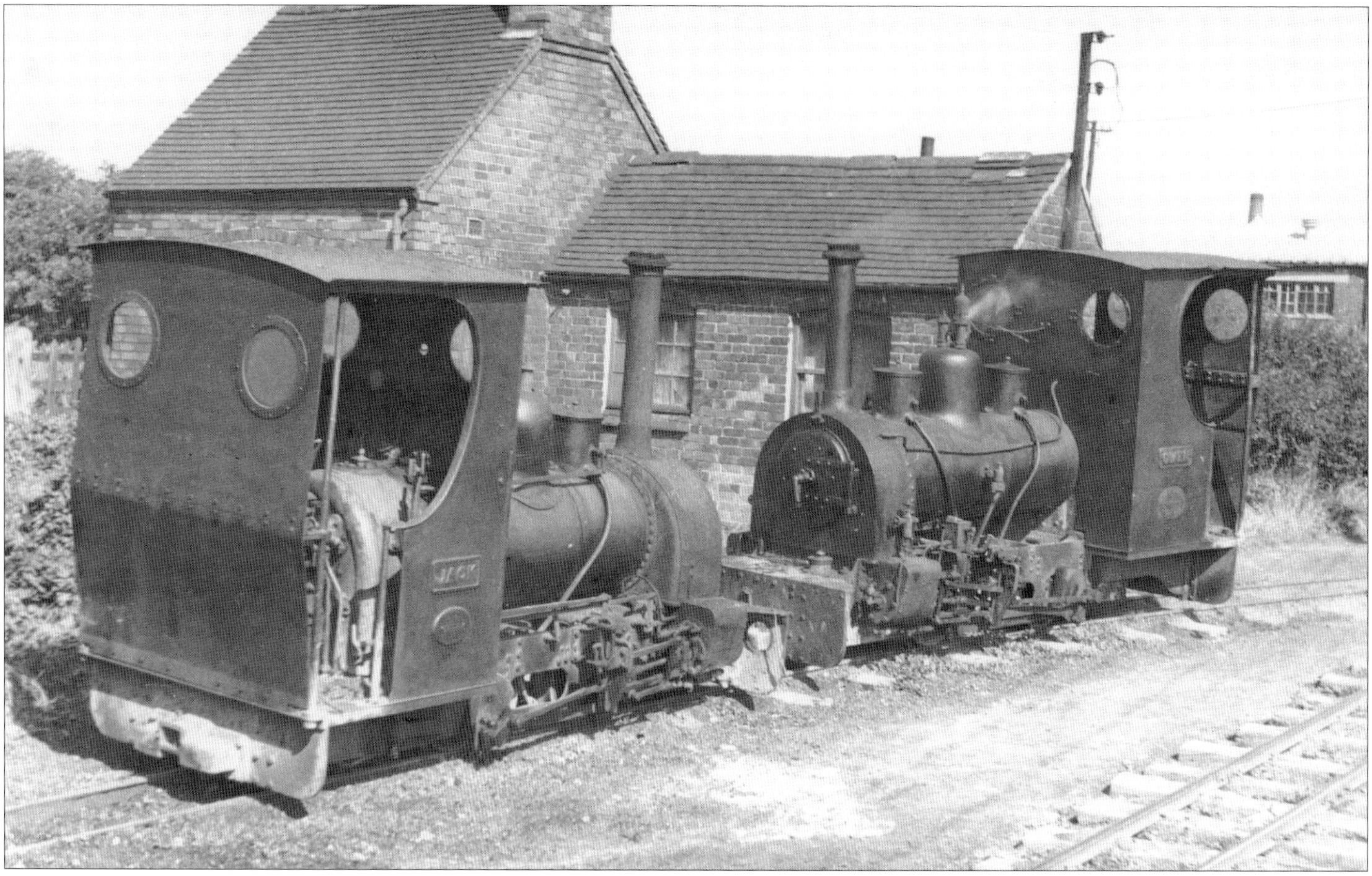

Knowles' *Jack* and *Gwen* chimney to chimney outside the locomotive shed at Woodville on 1st September 1953. *Jack* was out of steam and in store as the spare locomotive, as *Gwen* was the favoured locomotive after she arrived. [Maurice Billington, Peter Johnson collection]

Gwen in steam at John Knowles' railway with *Jack* out of steam behind on 27th March 1963. It is likely that in both pictures *Jack* has been hauled out of the shed for photographing at an enthusiast gathering. [Martin Fuller collection]

Hunslet 'frame tank' No. 12 (Works No. 1291 of 1917) seen with both Robert Hudson vehicles at Sand Hutton depot in 1927. George Batty, engineer, is seen driving No. 12 (although sometimes Sir Robert Walker himself also drove). The front buffer of the locomotive was slightly damaged after an altercation with a tree stump. The line's only passenger carriage was built in 1924 and had balconies at either end. It was painted in a burnt sienna livery with the initials 'SH' applied in brown edged gold lettering with a white roof; a very attractive vehicle and thankfully still in existence at the Lincolnshire Coast Light Railway. [PETER JOHNSON COLLECTION]

Sand Hutton Hunslet No. 12 with a passenger train, posed in the woods near Sand Hutton in 1927, with Sir Robert Walker looking on from behind a tree on the right. [PETER JOHNSON COLLECTION]

Esme on the five past one o'clock passenger train (Saturdays only) leaving Warthill for Bossall on 21st May 1927. [A.W. Croughton, Michael Whitehouse collection]

A short while later, *Esme* passes No. 12 at Warthill with the same train. [A.W. Croughton, Michael Whitehouse collection]

2
A CORNISH ENGINEMAN'S VIEW:
THE PENTEWAN RAILWAY
JOHN HENRY DREW (EDITED AND ABRIDGED)

The China Clay pit at St. Austell. The Pentewan Railway laboured with two persistent major handicaps: it never reached these clay pits, so the initial journey had to be made by road at greater expense and, even when the china clay reached Pentewan harbour by rail, the port suffered from silting up. As such, it was a poor second relation to nearby Charlestown, only really 'thriving' when the china clay business boomed for a short time, by taking the overspill traffic. [Neil Parkhouse collection]

I was born in Pentewan and lived there for the first twenty years of my life. I was a fireman on *Canopus* for six years, beginning in 1907 when I was 15 years of age, and the occasional driver on both that locomotive and *Pioneer*. My father worked on the railway as an engine driver for upwards of thirty years, from 1887. The railway and the harbour were closely linked and under the same management and the harbour master was also in charge of the railway and we took our orders from him. The practice followed was that each morning while the fireman was raising steam and getting the engine ready to leave the shed, Father would see the harbour master and get a general idea of what to do on each day. The task of carrying it out was then left mostly to the small staff that we were, and in particular, the engine driver as, after leaving St. Austell village, there was no means of communicating with us by phone or otherwise.

About a year after I joined Father on the engine, the port became busier; the pier was extended and the recurrent choking up of the entrance to the harbour by sand was prevented. This increased prosperity was very welcome, but it put a great strain on the *Canopus* as the only working engine. It was increasingly difficult to find time to keep her in repair and it was thought necessary to get a spare engine to act as a relief. When this engine arrived it proved to be not a new one, but an experimental 2-6-2T built for the War Office, a typical Government job, and by the look of her she had hardly been used, called the *Pioneer*. We considered her a poor buy.

The staff consisted of seven of us, two men at the St. Austell end, Jim Rickard the weighbridge man and Mac Grose the yard man. Jack Pearce the weighbridge and crossing man at Pentewan, the two engine men and Tom Marks and his ganger for the track. The port did at times employ a carpenter, mainly

China Clay workers group, St. Austell, posing for the photographer alongside a wooden tipping wagon at the foot of a rope worked incline. Everyone is wearing hats and a dog has joined the group for the photograph. [Neil Parkhouse collection]

Loading a wagon with China Clay. These wagons, delivered to the railway on its regauging to 2ft 6 inches, look as if they have an allegiance to Fell's designs as well as the steam locomotives, as they are also low slung. [Photographer unknown]

As the Pentewan Railway ran easily along the ground with no major earthworks, Fell did not need to use his patented elevated railway system for the main line, but brought it to bear to good effect for loading ships in the harbour at Pentewan. This picture gives clear view of the Fell designed raised wooden staithes at the harbour with two wagons perched on top. Chutes were provided for gravity loading into waiting ships. [Photographer unkown]

for repairing the trucks and viaduct; but when they were without one, Jack Pearce would render first aid. We would push those trucks requiring attention part way up the viaduct to enable him to get underneath to replace brake blocks which were of poplar wood bought ready made from Jury's sawmills, St. Austell.

The main bulk of traffic on the line was of course china clay down; the main up traffic was coal – steam, house and gas coal – but we also carried many other things including large quantities of grain wheat for Hitchen's flour mill at Blowing House, St. Austell (later replaced by imports of flour from Avonmouth for Gaved's store) and limestone for the kilns at Pentewan and St. Austell. There were also cargoes of cement, of staves for clay cask making for Vian & May at Polgooth and Phillips at Trewoon, of salt for Gaved's store, of vitriol and bones for Pentewan bone mill and occasional cargoes of wood hoops from France for the cooperage. There was an increasing export trade of sand towards the latter ends, for London and Plymouth mainly. This was taken by sailing barges.

At that time it was the custom for the clay works to load the waggons on the basis of first come first loaded. As there were frequently more wagons than loads, some waggoners would be at the clay dry at 4 or 5 o'clock in the morning to be certain of a load. If the clay dry was not more than two miles or so from the yard, they would do two loads a day or, occasionally, three, when we would have to wait for the last load if necessary to finish a cargo, and it would be six o'clock or more before we would get home to Pentewan.

When a vessel was ready to receive her cargo, the harbour master would write out the order and give it to Father to take up to Jim Rickard, the weighbridge man. He would carry it to the clay office concerned, as all the clay works had an office at St. Austell then. They would arrange the transportation to the yard. This was the most costly part of the journey as the waggoners used to get 2s 6d per ton where they could do two loads a day, whereas the port only charged 1s 0d a ton to carry it to Pentewan and put it aboard the boat. The coaster would get as freight from 2s 6d, 2s 9d, sometimes 3s 0d a ton. This latter was a good freight, as they used to reckon to carry clay as a paying ballast to get to the coal ports such as Runcorn or the Bristol Channel to make their profit, if any, on coal.

When I was a schoolboy, Jack Pearce's son, Henry Arthur Pearce, who was my age, would after school get as many of us boys as he could to help him fill the water tank, which was fine fun for us playing with the pump. The engine used to fill up with water before starting each trip up. After weighing our load we would move a bit further along to the water tank and, while Father oiled the connecting, bearing and motion gear, I would fill the engine tank. In a full day's work the *Canopus* would use 4-500 gallons of water and about 5-6 cwt of coal. Our coal was stored in a shed just below the engine shed, and after our first round after dinner we would fill up her bunker while waiting for enough trucks to be tipped for our last trip that day. The port would have 50 tons of coal at a time as part cargo with some other merchant and that amount would last us quite a while.

We used to draw the fire every night, as it was found that owing to the depth and shape of the firebox it paid to light up afresh each morning with a clean firebox, except when we worked late when it wasn't worth it. This gave Jack Pearce another job each

View of Pentewan harbour around 1906. The railway ran round both sides of the basin and, on the left of the view, can be seen the raised wooden trestle section designed by John Barraclough Fell; even today an elevated section here can still be seen. The trestles were largely later filled in by concrete embankments, although the effect was similar. The railway on the right-hand side of the harbour, viewed from where the photographer was standing, ran round in front of the buildings and two wagons loaded with coal can be seen alongside the sailing ship.
[Neil Parkhouse collection]

A Sunday school outing with *Trewithen* fully loaded with families excited by their unusual day out. *Trewithen* was the second Manning, Wardle 0-6-0 tender locomotive for the line, replacing *Pentewan* once she wore out. As only one locomotive was needed to run the service, there was no need to order a new tender and she ran using *Pentewan*'s, but was provided with a commodious cab which *Pentewan* lacked.
[Photographer unknown]

day, to split up old sleepers to light the fire in the mornings. The fireman was supposed to light the fire, but Father used to do this for me while I ate my breakfast and, while Father was having his breakfast, I would keep the fire going, fill up sand boxes and draw oil into cans for engine and trucks. It usually took about an hour each day after Monday to raise steam. Mondays would take longer as she would be cold over the weekend. It took 60lbs of steam to get the *Canopus* out of the house in the morning.

The *Canopus* would take about fifteen minutes up or down all the way. We normally made four trips a day to West Bridge or 'Up Yard' as we used to say. We made our first trip up about 8.30am, the second about 11am, third 2pm and the last at 4pm. I have known making five or six trips up a day, especially when we had to work the Sunday School outings from St. Austell to Pentewan and back.

Most running repairs had to be done by the driver and his mate. With all the enforced practice Father had, what with repairs to the engine and working the forge, he became quite a useful blacksmith and fitter, which was a great credit to him as he never went to school. For the *Canopus* we had a spare set of motion gear, which Father would change and use alternately while one set was sent to the makers at Leeds for refreshing and general overhaul. As regards the main driving and connecting rod bearings, Father would when necessary take them apart, adjust them to take up the wear, and reassemble them.

The railway always employed a working ganger. He worked mostly by himself, but when the port was slack he could, if required, have spare men from the quay to help relay parts of the line. The coming of the *Pioneer* with her narrow tyred wheels made the relaying programme more urgent and more difficult for the ganger, with limited resources to keep the track in fair condition. The track, in fact, was in some places shocking. I have seen an old fashioned chair rail fly up one end and down again when the engine struck the other end. Father always carried dogs and a navvy's hammer on the engine, as we often had to stop and do a bit of repairing where the rails had spread. We carried two jacks, together with blocks of wood for getting her back on the line, and two short pieces of rail pointed at one end for slocking trucks back again when they left the line. The *Canopus* had two whistles, one rough and the other soft. It was the custom that when within earshot of the Pentewan end, if all was well, Father would sound the soft one; but if we were in distress he would use the rough one and the men would come to aid us.

Another Sunday School outing before 1908 with *Canopus* at Iron Bridge loop. These outings were very popular at the time, but it was very rough riding, with trucks packed to capacity, the line a bit bumpy, and the bramble bushes on the sides of the line not too well trimmed. Quite a few would lose their hats, which were often found next day and left at the weighbridge at St. Austell to be called for.
[Photographer unknown]

Steam ship Foy discharging coal into trucks in Pentewan harbour, giving a good view of the three plank wooden wagons and their side buffers. The wagons took on a different colour, depending whether they are loaded with china clay or coal. Probably the whole schoolboy population of the town is on the ship enjoying the antics of the cameraman who would have set up his tripod to take the glass plate picture in around 1905. [Neil Parkhouse collection]

The Pentewan Railway was originally horse worked and possibly 4ft 6 inch gauge, but in 1873, the Pentewan Railway & Harbour Co. Ltd was incorporated and the line relaid to 2ft 6 inch gauge under a contract placed with John Barraclough Fell. Manning, Wardle were contracted to deliver this lovely and unusual 0-6-0 tender engine named *Pentewan*, built with a very low slung boiler and seen here on the harbour wooden staging around 1880. The locomotive was built to Fell's design for use on his system of railways built using timber trestles that could be erected simply and cheaply across uneven ground; the low centre of gravity was an essential requirement for its rolling stock. This system never got beyond the experimental stage. [JOHN ALSOP COLLECTION]

Canopus at St. Austell surrounded by china clay. This was the transshipment point for the road haulage section from the mine to the train for the journey onwards to Pentewan harbour. [JOHN ALSOP COLLECTION]

Pentewan did not last overlong and was replaced by a similar locomotive named *Trewithin*, but in the 'good times' for the harbour and the railway, a stronger locomotive was clearly needed. *Canopus*, a sturdy 0-6-2T (unusually with the trailing wheels the same size as the driving wheels), was delivered in 1901, again built by Manning, Wardle and painted in emerald green with red and yellow lining. She is seen here in 1912 standing on Fell's wooden harbour trestles at Pentewan. [JOHN ALSOP COLLECTION]

Canopus seen here on the outskirts of Pentewan, shunting a single china clay wagon on what was clearly washing day. [JOHN ALSOP COLLECTION]

A Cornish Engineman's View: The Pentewan Railway

ABOVE AND BELOW: *Pioneer*, an ex-War Department 2-6-2T, built by the Yorkshire Engine Co. for the Lodge Hill & Upnor Railway, arrived in 1912 as a spare locomotive for *Canopus*. She was also built as an experiment, combining outside bar and plate frames, Belpair firebox and fitted with oil firing and a very scanty cab. She was more 'highly strung' and rather unsuited to a rather roughly kept china clay line; she would have been more at home romping away on a passenger railway. No doubt the harbour and railway's then owner, Mrs Johnstone, bought her as she was probably cheap, but more importantly available in the correct track gauge. She is seen here paired with Mrs Johnstone's Director's coach which was only ever used for owner's trips on the line, which were almost a state occasion, and otherwise spent its life slumbering at the back of the locomotive shed. [JOHN ALSOP COLLECTION/PHOTOGRAPHER UNKNOWN]

Canopus with a fully loaded train of china clay at the Iron Bridge loop. [Photograper unknown]

We very often had a passenger or two up to St. Austell or back on the footplate. Others would ride on the trucks as well. Of course it was all free. The port estate, including the railway, passed to the Johnstone family and her son George started the custom of driving periodically in their horse carriage from Trewithen to West Bridge terminal to ride in the Director's railway carriage down to Pentewan. This entailed making a special journey up and back, meeting them at the St. Austell end about 1pm. It was my job each time to give the carriage a good clean out, as between trips it was used as a storage place for cotton waste. The routine was always the same: Father would step off the footplate, open the carriage door and touch his cap, while Mrs Johnstone would say "*Good morning, Drew*". When we arrived at Pentewan, Father would open the door for them to get out. Her remark this time was invariable. "*Thank you, Drew, a very pleasant ride*". Mrs Johnstone and her son would then have lunch with the harbour master. We would carry on with our normal work until later in the afternoon when we would return them to St. Austell. These trips were regarded by the staff as rather a nuisance as they hindered the work, and there was the risk of derailing them, although we never did. Maybe it would have paid to have got them off a time or two; perhaps they would have improved the track.

Almost all that is remembered of the line today [1960] is the Sunday School outings in the summer. These were very popular at the time, but I doubt whether under present day conditions of recreation they would be. It was very rough riding, with trucks packed to capacity, the line a bit bumpy, and the bramble bushes on the sides of the line not too well trimmed. Quite a few would lose their hats, which we often found next day and would leave at the weighbridge at St. Austell to be called for. The proprietors of the harbour granted the trips free to all the chapels and churches of St. Austell, but the Sunday Schools had to give the railway staff an extra day's pay to cover the trips and time in the evening to return them to St. Austell. The Sunday Schools used to charge a shilling for grown ups, which covered the tea on the Winnick [grass covered area by the sands] and the trip down and back, but of course for the children it was all free.

It was all so free and easy that, if we could manage the extra load, a couple of extra trucks were sometimes put on in the evenings for the Pentewan and Mevagissey people to make the round trip and join in the fun.

The *Canopus* had to pull as many as sixteen or seventeen trucks in returning the Church Sunday School to the town. After a hard pull up to town I had to clean out the *Canopus* smokebox which would get full of ashes when pulling heavy. She had a very strong exhaust and threw out hot ashes which some people who had not been on the trip before would get in their eyes.

'*But what a violent pleasure it was: we couldn't have been more excited and tingling with expectancy if we were making a journey into Darkest Africa. And actually when we left the obviousness of the roadway behind us and the track took us beside the river skirting King's Wood, the river might have been the Limpopo and the wood the equatorial forest, it was all so exotic and thrilling. The overhanging vegetation plucked your cap off before you knew where you were; the dragon flies darted gorgeously by on the wing; the honey suckles reached their fingers into the truck and tickled your neck; there was a rank vegetation of every sort of flower, yellow and purple and red, alongside the track; there were moorhens flitting in and out of the flags of the swamps; and as we arrived at our destination, the little ponds that fed the dock basin were the splendidest of lakes. We paddled. We ran about the Winnick and then we had tea: each of us an enormous, round, golden, saffron bun, corrugated with currants and flavoured with lemon peel. When at the end of a day's racing about on the beach, we were gathered once more into the trucks, on our return journey through the woods, darkening and mysterious with evening, there was. Quieter mood prevailing. We sang.*
I celebrate those outings to Pentewan at length, for they have long since ceased. When the War came the little track was taken up – to be laid again in who knows what battlefields of France or Palestine? – the trucks and the engine dispersed. It ended the prosperity of the little harbour, and the ships came there less and less. But for us, it meant perhaps more; it was the end of an epoch, the end of childhood.' [A.W. Rouse]

Opposite page top: Line drawing of *Ariel* and her tender sitting on elevated wooden trestles. A writer in *The Engineer* commented sarcastically '*as a means of the construction of an expensive and ridiculous form of permanent way, and a type of locomotive having no practical advantages, Mr Fell's plan is admirable*'. Arthur Heywood described the line as '*a sad failure*', but Fell had the last laugh over Heywood in gaining construction work elsewhere.

Opposite page centre: Line drawing of *Pentewan* which shows the similarity with *Ariel* except that it did not have the low hanging cylinders or side guidance wheels as these were unnecessary for a railway laid on the ground. Probably Manning, Wardle were asked to build *Pentewan* as they had first built *Ariel*.

Opposite page bottom: *Marland*, an 0-6-0 side tank, was built by Bagnall in 1883, with works No. 566 for the Torrington & Marland Railway. Note the nine foot long wheelbase of the 6-coupled wheels designed to spread the weight over Fell's timber viaducts. In this respect, all three locomotives, each influenced by Fell, were similar.

A Cornish Engineman's View: The Pentewan Railway

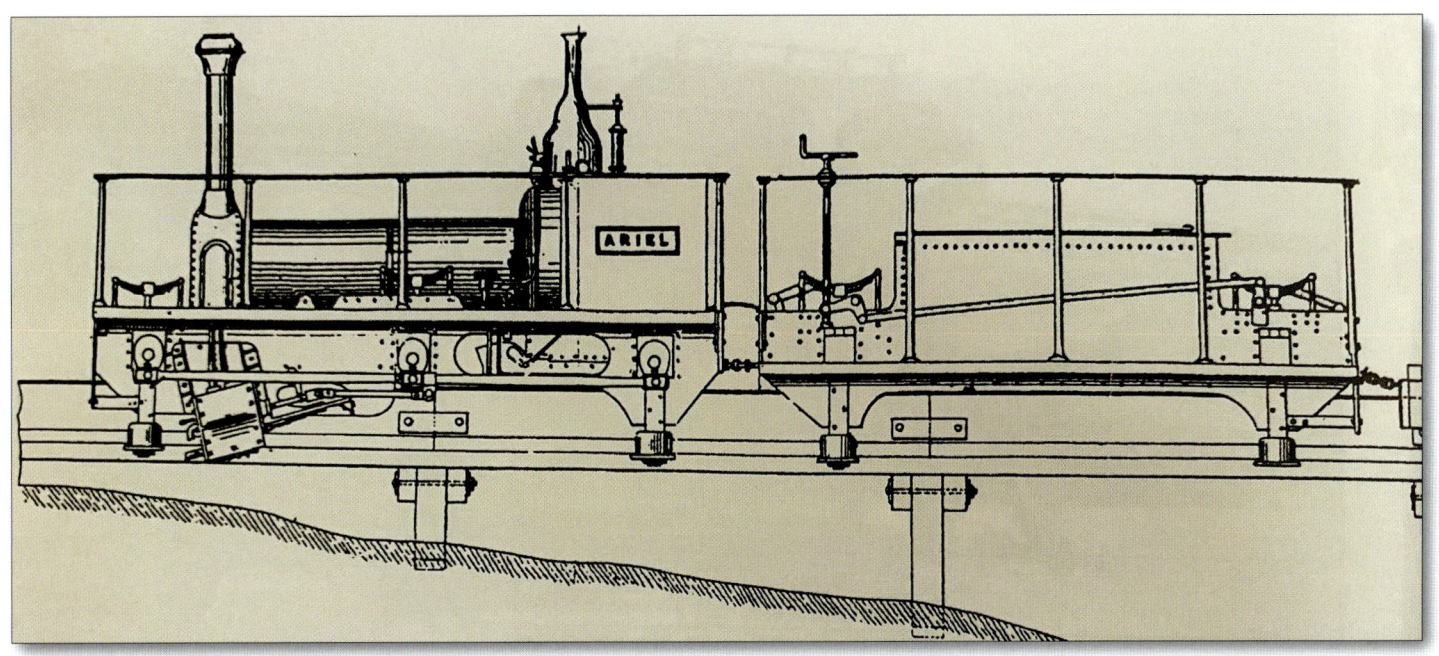

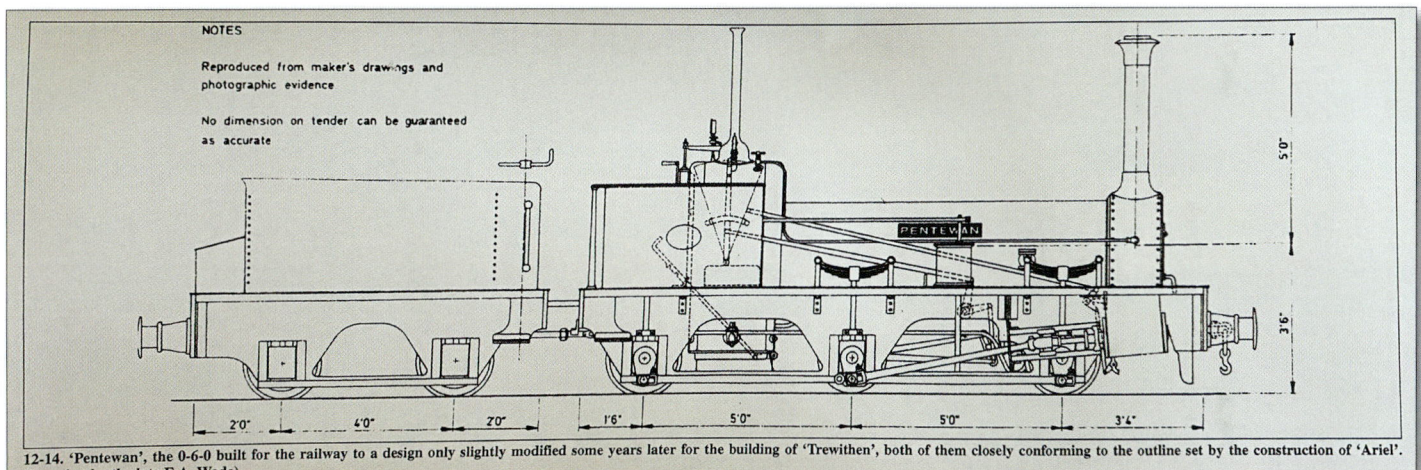

12-14. 'Pentewan', the 0-6-0 built for the railway to a design only slightly modified some years later for the building of 'Trewithen', both of them closely conforming to the outline set by the construction of 'Ariel'. (Drawing by the late E.A. Wade)

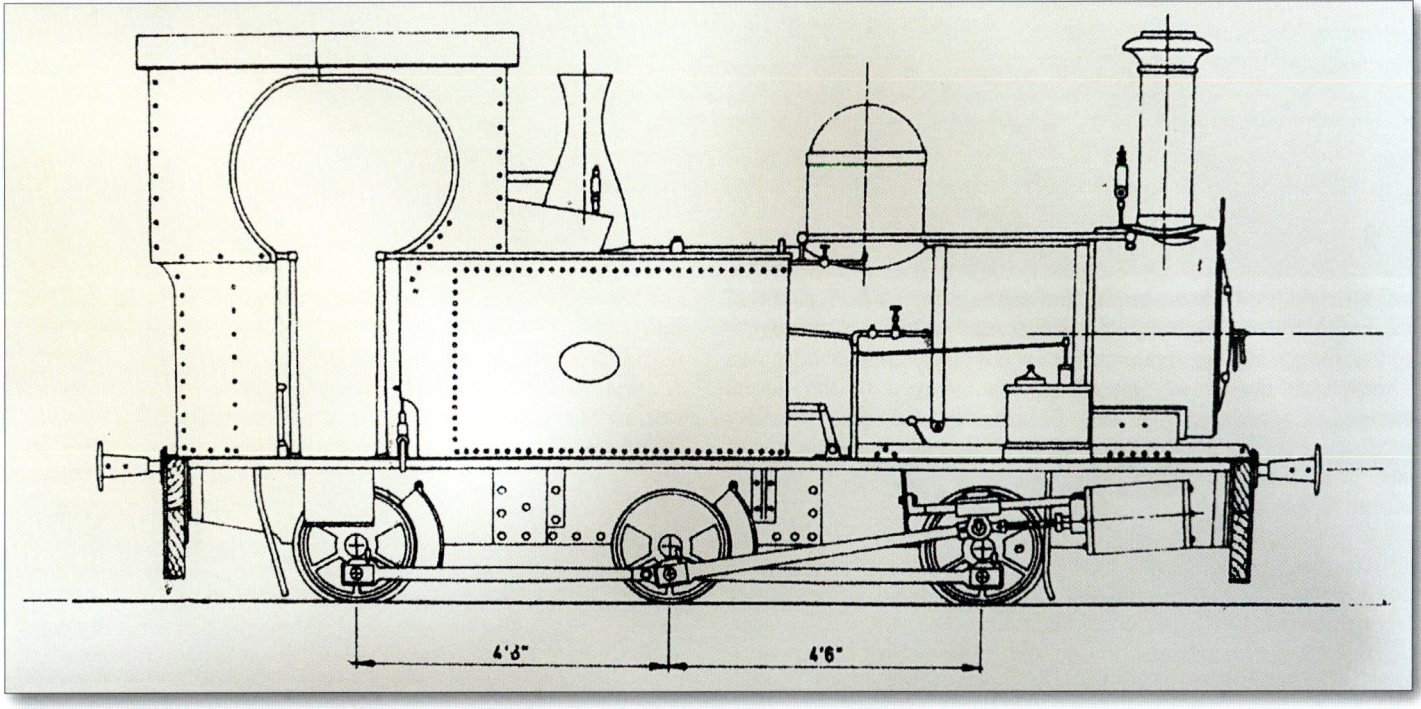

The classic view of the River Torridge at Torrington, looking from the western edge of Great Torrington Common circa 1900. A popular viewpoint with postcard publishers, it thus ensured that the T&MR's distinctive wooden viaduct was well photographed for posterity. The line headed into the cutting on the right and then curved round beneath Station Hill to enter the goods yard at Torrington station, in the right background. [Neil Parkhouse collection]

3
OUTPACED BY DEMAND:
THE TORRINGTON & MARLAND RAILWAY

'At 12 o'clock precisely the whistle blew, and the small party were taken at once gently through a short tunnel, some of them raising a faint cheer. On emerging, however, and getting onto the slender looking bridge, right above the river Torridge, and from thence onto a timber viaduct, 266 yards in length, and forty feet in height, the feeling of jollity suddenly changed to one of wonder and tremulation – wonder that engineering skill could devise so light a structure combined with safety, and tremulation lest the one thought uppermost in the minds of all should be realised. A looker-on from the common above afterwards informed us that the movement of the train across the viaduct as he looked down upon it presented the appearance of a party of children being conveyed across a toy bridge in perambulators. As steam was put on, and we rattled along on what was, comparatively speaking, on terra firma, round the thickly wooded slopes, reassurance returned, only to leave us again on finding ourselves on a viaduct crossing a narrow gorge dividing a most picturesque and well studded wood. In fact the scenery through which the line passes from beginning to end is of such a character as can rarely be seen from any railway in England.
By and by, noticing that Mr Fell himself was at the front, and that the engine was under the complete control of the driver and then reflecting that Mount Cenis had been conquered by this same skilful engineer with his light railway, all qualms died away.'
[Bideford Weekly Gazette]

This cruel enlargement from a circa 1908 distant view of the L&SWR's Torrington Branch terminus station provides a rare glimpse of the narrow gauge T&MR siding running in between two standard gauge sidings on the east side of the goods yard. A couple of narrow gauge opens can be seen with their clay loads being transshipped into standard gauge wagons alongside. The T&MR line entered the yard through the gate just discernible between the goods shed and the box van at the end of the siding. [JOHN ALSOP COLLECTION]

On 15th February, 1882, the North Devon town of Marland received a visit from a man wearing traditional Chinese attire and with a pig tail. Mr Fung Yee caused quite a stir being the first Chinese man the townsfolk had ever seen. Mr Lee was the Secretary of the Chinese Legation in London and he had come to the town to see the new railway, built in 1881. The Chinese Legation had been established in 1877 and the London mission was China's first permanent overseas diplomatic mission, originally for the Manch Qing Empire and, since 1950, for the People's Republic of China.

Accompanying Mr Lee was Major Grover, RE, of the British War Office. The Japanese Ambassador was also expected, but was unfortunately prevented from joining by other

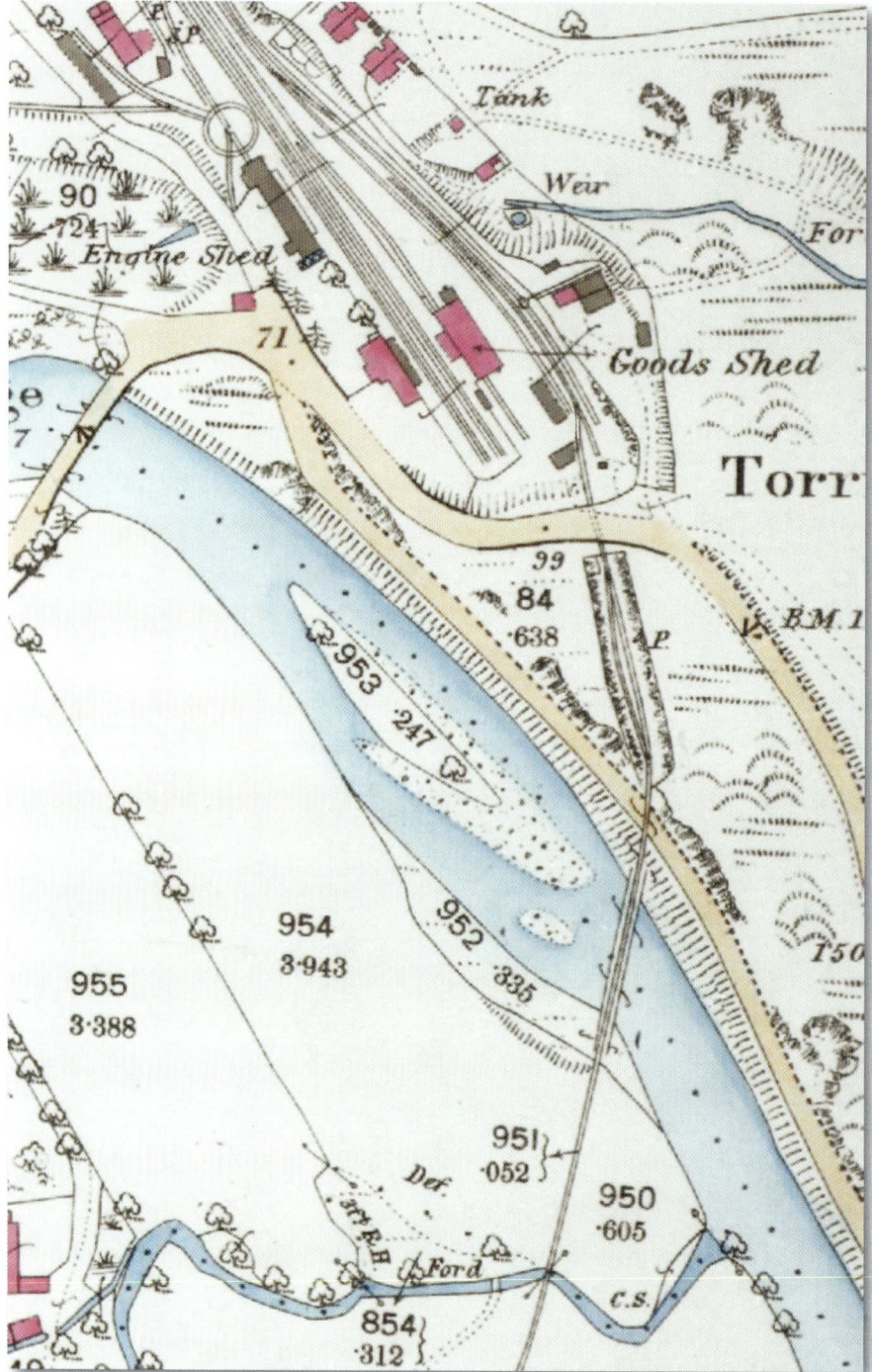

This extract from the 25 inch OS of 1886 (published in 1887) shows the arrangement of the narrow and standard gauge lines at Torrington station. Also shown is the run round loop situated in the cutting, illustrated by the picture on the next page.

using wooden viaducts to save excavation costs, monorail systems with gripping wheels and his own centre rail system for mountain railways; the Snaefell Mountain Railway in the Isle of Man still uses this invention. Quite rightly, he advocated the use of low-cost construction methods and (aligned in his thinking generally with Richard Rapier in East Anglia who we will meet later), he addressed the Liverpool Engineering Society on 11th September, 1878 showing that most railways (other than main line trunk routes) were unable to earn more than the percentage dividends on their preference shares or loan capital, leaving no return for ordinary shareholders, other than the amenity created by having the railway built. This is a theme which will recur in relation to most of the narrow gauge lines in this book, other than purely industrial concerns built to serve a single mineral purpose.

In the 16th century, the port of Bideford grew as a consequence of its direct connection with the British Colonies in North America, particularly in relation to the tobacco trade founded by Sir Walter Raleigh, then only exceeded by the Port of London. Ships also traded in every day necessities for the colonials and a demand for pottery saw substantial quantities purchased from the clay deposits in the region. A white clay was found nearby around Marland which had a role as a decorative material and also for making clay pipes for making smoking tobacco. The clay deposits were and still are enormous and now find uses as an inert filler in animal foodstuffs, fertilisers, paint, runner

commitments. These gentleman had come to look at John Barraclough Fell's new railway. The Chinese Government were considering the use of light railways to open up their country and Major Grover had already inspected Fell's experimental 18 inch gauge railway laid down at Aldershot (which we discussed in the Minimum Gauge essay) and had come to see Fell's improvements.

As we have already seen, Fell had made a railway career building railways in many parts of the world and had good connections: he distinguished himself by creating the first mountain railway to begin operations in the world in 1868, climbing over the Mont Cenis Pass between France and Italy. He spent much time on railway experiments and had filed patents for various inventions for low cost railway construction

and plastics. The clay was also used to make bricks. The Lynton & Barnstaple Railway's Chelfham viaduct is a fine example of the use of Marland bricks.

The Greening and Wren families owned the relevant land and William Wren, JP, began trial workings around 1876-78 when he built kilns and industrial buildings at his new Marland Brick & Tile Works. He developed the business from 1897 and invested £25,000, which demonstrated this was no 'fly by night' operation, to connect the Works to the outside world at Torrington. This facilitated the transfer goods to the London & South Western Railway. The mine owners may well have come across Fell's Liverpool address to its engineering society, but anyway, the two connected and planning began.

There was little difficulty in gaining the necessary consents

Telegrams: "Holwill, Torrington."
Telephone No. 10.

Torrington, Jany 1st 1919

Mr. Hayward Hartleigh Buckland Filleigh Dolton

To The North Devon Clay Compy., Ltd.

(The Torrington and Marland Light Railway).

Carriage Account.

				T.	C.	Q.	lbs.			
1918 Mar 4	Manure	Bury Mon	ex W.C.A	4				4/6	18	0

7L159

LEFT: A carriage account from the Torrington & Marland Light Railway for public traffic.

BELOW: The 0-6-0T *Avonside* backs onto a train in the loop just outside Torrington station with the Torridge viaduct in the background. Crossing this enormous viaduct some 30ft about the surrounding fields must have been quite an experience, as recounted by the *Bideford Weekly Gazette* at the head of this essay, since the train would have been at least equal in width to the wooden trestle bridge and passengers sitting in the wagons must have felt suspended in mid-air whilst being jolted along.
[JOHN ALSOP COLLECTION]

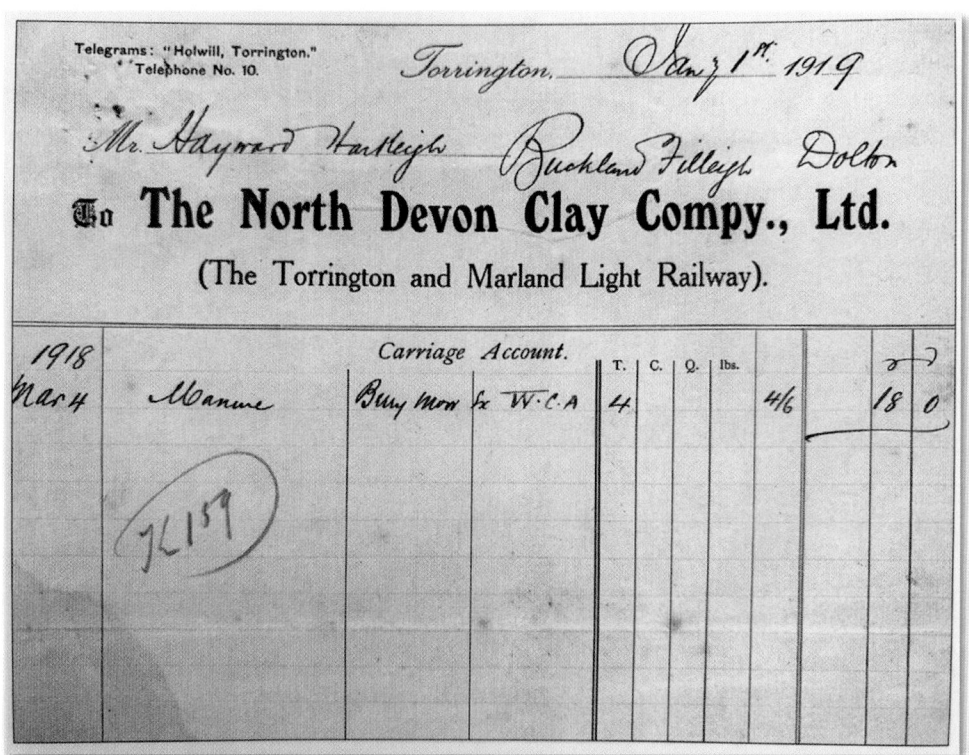

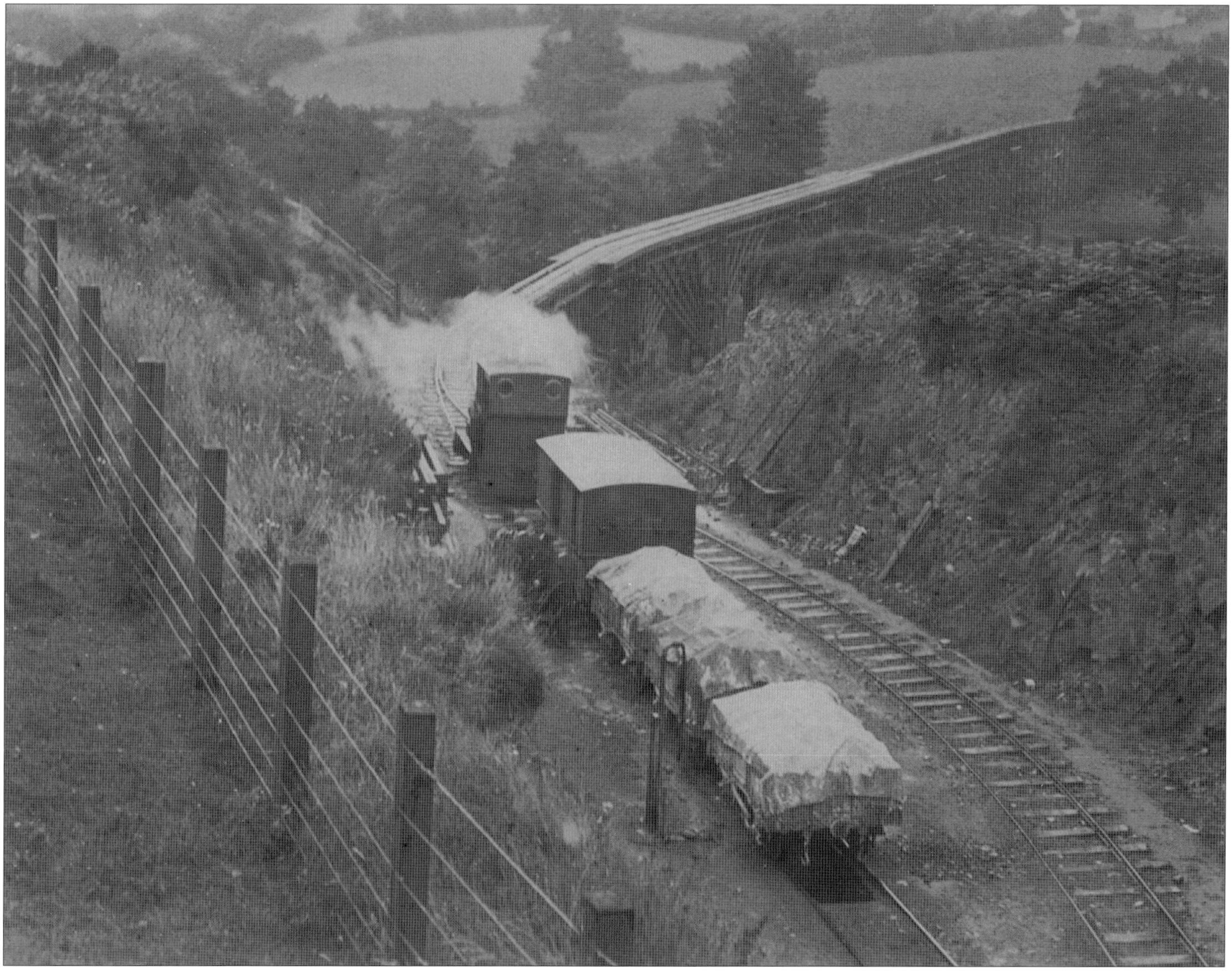

Black, Hawthorn & Co. 0-6-0T *Mary* hauls a workmens' train, comprising the two former London County Council horse tramcars and two converted open wagons, across the Rolle Road after leaving Torrington in around 1910. *Mary* was most probably named after Fell's son George's wife, who officiated in cutting the first sod on the railway at Torrington station on Wednesday, 20th May 1880. Sadly, Mary died before the opening ceremony. [JOHN ALSOP COLLECTION]

ABOVE: *Mary*, running cab first, brings a late afternoon mixed train over the Torridge viaduct. The train includes two of the wagons converted for passenger use and one of the London tramcars, although clearly some of the workers still preferred to ride in the open wagons. [JOHN ALSOP COLLECTION]

The permanent way, demonstrating John Barraclough Fell's concept of a railway, designed to be cheap and economical but still capable of efficiently handling the clay traffic required. [NEIL PARKHOUSE COLLECTION]

ABOVE AND BELOW: *Jersey 1*, an 0-4-0T built in 1873 by Fletcher Jennings (Works No. 129), came originally from St. Helier's breakwater in Jersey. As 3ft gauge steam locomotives were uncommon in Britain, the opportunity was taken to buy three tank locomotives from Jersey in 1908. All three arrived as 0-4-0 saddle tanks but were rebuilt here at Peters Marland in 1910. These photographs were taken between 1920-25 and show the locomotive carrying around its saddle tank as a tender, an ingenious solution to solving the weight problem these second-hand acquisitions caused. [MARTIN FULLER COLLECTION]

from local landowners, which avoided the need for an expensive Act of Parliament. Fell was appointed to survey the route and then as engineer in June 1880. Fell's company, Greenodd Railway & General contracting Company Limited, were appointed to build the railway at a price of £10,580 within seven months. Greenodd, in Cumbria, was the Fell family home. He saw this railway as an opportunity to put some of his beliefs into practice and also use it as a demonstration ground hopefully for new business. However, although the railway he built was suitable for the clay traffic, neither the Chinese nor the Army (or for that matter the Japanese) saw fit to adopt his principles in their subsequent railway construction.

The railway was specifically designed to be fit for purpose: cheap and economical and required only to handle the clay traffic. It was simply built to a three foot gauge with single line, passing loops and sidings only where needed, no signalling or stations and only minimal earthworks. It had one special distinguishing feature though, and this had drawn the Chinese and War Office visitors to come and look. This was the use of a series of long wooden viaducts instead of embankments and bridges which were the subject of patents taken out by Fell. His idea was to avoid the 'cut and fill' principle of conventional railway construction where material excavated from cuttings is used to fill valleys and depressions. Instead, Fell advocated laying track directly onto the ground and, where embankments would normally have been constructed, using long wooden girders, supported on wooden or iron frames, to carry the railway over the ground. His concept included prefabricating this structure for speedy erection on site. As we have already seen, he had also gained the contract for rebuilding the Pentewan Railway in Cornwall and converting it to 2ft 6 inch gauge but, as this was simply laid on a gradual gradient down to the harbour, there was no need for wooden viaducts.

The Torrington and Marland Railway, however, enabled Fell actually to use his wooden structures as this new railway ran through undulating countryside and, somewhat naturally for Fell, he took out yet more patents to cover the specific design. These unique viaducts were most distinctive, as can be seen in the pictures. Wooden viaducts were, of course, common in Victorian times, but Fell's were different to, say, Brunel's well-known structures. Brunel and other engineers commonly used supports radiating from their bases like a fan, but Fell's supports were mostly straight forward verticals at right angles to the railway, with strengthening fan-like diagonal stays to give greater strength and stability. They were certainly successful on the T&MR as they lasted with, probably, minimal maintenance for over forty years. Certainly also, his construction methods worked as regards time and cost. The six-mile railway was completed within the time specified in the contract and was still economically built (although he did overrun the tendered price). One consequence of his methods was that the steam locomotives ordered for the line had long wheelbases so as to spread their weight on the timber structures, but he abandoned his predilection with lateral guiding wheels and, instead, relied on the three foot gauge as being slightly wider than his previous experimental lines.

Of course, the railway was built for a single source of freight traffic and not passengers. So, it was unsurprising that in reporting the opening of the railway in 1881, journalists related that riding in 4-wheeled open wagons was not as smooth as might be experienced in a superior horse drawn carriage. On New Year's Day in that year, a train load of Marland bricks made a first journey and the opening ceremony, postponed to 5th February, on account of snow, enabled Fell to take the Mayors of Torrington and Barnstaple, local landowners and the press over the railway by train, followed by a sumptuous dinner at the Globe Hotel in Torrington at Fell's expense.

The railway was operated in two halves, each on the 'one engine in steam' principle, divided at the summit loop. Two short trains of four full wagons each would be worked to the summit from the works, then to be made up into an eight-wagon train for the remainder of the journey to Torrington, with locomotives being exchanged at the summit.

The railway itself only needed three locomotives, although a fourth was obtained in 1900. *Mary* was a Black, Hawthorn & Co. Ltd 0-6-0ST, *Marland*, an 0-6-0 side tank, was built by Bagnall and the third was an Avonside 0-6-0ST which was given the nickname of its builder. The fourth locomotive was also an Avonside with similarities to *Mary*. There were several other smaller locomotives within the yards at the mine, including three bought from Jersey, a Stephen Lewin 0-4-0T and a 'coffeepot'. The railway had 49 wagons, initially, all built by Metropolitan Railway Carriage & Wagon Co. of Birmingham; a substantial number due to the considerable expansion of the clay workings. As well as this, the railway also provided a common carrier service as required along the line, except for livestock or timber which the wagons could not realistically handle, although there was an undoubted demand for carrying such traffic. Whilst mine workers and also members of the public travelled in the open wagons, the railway first converted some of these into makeshift vans, then, in 1909, acquired a couple of redundant tram bodies from London County Council who were converting from horse power to electrification.

The brick and clay business receipts rose and fell according to business demand and was of course affected by the world wars, then booms and depressions in economy. The business continues to this day, albeit under Belgian ownership and the scale of operations is larger than it has ever been. The railway, albeit then powered by Ruston diesel locomotives, but only within the mine area, lasted until 1971, when the mining methodology changed to open cast and road vehicles were brought in to service the ever changing working face of an expanding quarry.

The three-foot main line railway itself was ousted by a standard gauge competitor in 1925. This takeover had roots as far back as 1831, when plans were discussed for a railway connecting Torrington and Okehampton, followed by various other schemes, but none came to fruition. Whilst Fell's railway satisfied the needs of the Marland clay workings, it did little for the rest of the region, in particular the prosperous town of Hatherleigh to the south. In the 1890s various schemes were promoted to connect Torrington with the L&SWR line to the south, but it was Holman F. Stephens, of considerable light railway fame, who lit the final touch paper.

Following the Royal Assent of the Light Railways Act, 1898, Stephens came up with the concept of a light railway in North Devon using all the powers that legislation provided

to encourage the public sector to participate. Stephens initially began with the concept of laying a third rail along the Torrington & Marland Railway. However, he quickly found this idea would not work, after inspecting the Torridge viaduct in 1909 which he determined would not take the weight of a standard gauge wagon, let alone a train. By the end of that year, however, his plans were sufficiently advanced to make a Light Railway Order application. He failed to come to financial terms to buy the T&MR, so forged ahead to build a parallel standard gauge railway instead. He persuaded the Devon County Council and local councils to subscribe for shares and applied for a Treasury grant, as permitted by the Act, but the First World War intervened. However, the light railway powers already granted were kept in being until peace resumed and then the political pressure to build this new railway increased, although Sir Herbert Walker, the L&SWR General Manager took the view that such a railway could not be made to pay and that he would require a guarantee of 100

An almost full view of John Barraclough Fell's spectacular Torridge viaduct. Fell's creations were very distinctive in their design and certainly successful on the Torrington & Marland as they lasted, with probably minimal maintenance, for over forty years. Fell used Baltic pine with supports being mostly straight forward verticals at right angles to the railway, but also with strengthening fan like diagonal stays to give greater strength and stability – not unlike Brunel's designs for the Great Western Railway. As already noted, the river spans were commonly photographed but the far longer section crossing the valley – comprising closely spaced simple upright wooden piers – is seldom seen. When the line was rebuilt to standard gauge, opening in 1925 as the North Devon & Cornwall Junction Light Railway, the new viaduct had to similarly span the whole of the Torridge flood plain. The workmen in the right foreground appear to be digging out the shallow river bed to aid water flow. [JOHN ALSOP COLLECTION]

per cent of gross receipts if his railway was to agree to do so.

David Lloyd George's government were keen for a project to deliver their light railway policies and also relieve unemployment; it was even agreed that, despite the advent of road motors which were now making incursions into rural railway traffic, a railway was necessary to deal with the likely volume of demand. Stephens was clearly master of his objective and, eventually, he succeeded in obtaining the agreement of the T&MR to sell for £18,000, he convinced its owners to take a proportion in shares in the new railway, gained increased local authority financial support and a contribution of up to £125,000 from the Ministry of Transport, together with agreement from the L&SWR to work the line for 75 per cent of gross receipts. No mean feat! Almost certainly, the factor swinging the government behind the project was the agreement to use unskilled labour on the new construction (honoured more in the breach rather than the observance). During the construction of the standard gauge line, it was agreed that the clay traffic on the three foot railway would have priority and not be severed, and it seems this was largely achieved. The new railway was approved by the Ministry of Transport and the L&SWR began to work it in July 1925. The townsfolk of Hatherleigh had the railway they wanted. But 'of course' it did not survive Beeching and now a heritage preservation group have reopened Torrington as the Tarka Valley Railway.

But Fell had delivered and Stephens' skills took the development of the railway on to the next stage. Oh, that he had also been involved in improving L'al Ratty and upgrading the Southwold lines, but perhaps there he would have failed with both, as the iron ore reserves in Cumbria were weak and competition from other ports and railway in Suffolk was strong, as we shall see in the next essays.

The 0-6-0T No. 2 *Marland*, built by Wm Bagnall in 1883, Works No. 566, was scrapped in 1925. Note the unusual and large safety valve in front of the cab and the tallow kettle hanging from a bracket on the smokebox, enabling tallow to be warmed to enable the locomotive and train to be lubricated. All Torrington & Marland locomotives were painted in unlined dark green and all three of the main line locomotives were 6-coupled with a long 9ft wheelbase to spread the weight over Fell's timber viaducts. [JOHN ALSOP COLLECTION]

Another view of the 0-6-0T No. 2 *Marland*, taken on the same day. [JOHN ALSOP COLLECTION]

The North Devon & Cornwall Junction Light Railway was a line promoted to connect the standard gauge terminus at Torrington to Halwill Junction, where the routes to Bude and Launceston diverged. Although all of these lines were owned and operated by the London & South Western Railway, the ND&CJLR was independent and remained so until Nationalisation. Construction began in the summer of 1921 but the original contractor, P&W Anderson Ltd of Glasgow, went bankrupt in early 1925 before the line was finished. The work was completed under the auspices of Colonel Holman F. Stephens and the line was operated by the Southern Railway when it finally opened on 27th July 1925. Its main traffic was in the carriage of ball clay from clay pits along its route but a passenger service was also operated, albeit one that was mostly used by clay workers. The new line was standard gauge and involved conversion of the T&MR between Meeth and Torrington. However, the contractor, Andersons, worked with 3ft gauge stock and their locomotive *Bunty* is seen here with a rake of side tipping spoil wagons being loaded by a Ruston steam shovel. *Bunty* was an 0-4-0ST built by Bagnalls of Stafford in 1896 (Works No. 1480), which had previously worked with the Scottish contractor Sir John Jackson. Its fate after its work here on the ND&CJLR was finished is unknown. [JOHN ALSOP COLLECTION]

Although the line between the clay pits and Torrington was rebuilt as part of the standard gauge ND&CJLR, the railway system at Peters Marland continued to be narrow gauge. This Fowler 'Resilient' Class 4-wheeled diesel-mechanical, Works No. 3900012 of 1947, was less than a year old when this picture was taken. The company named the locomotive *Forward* and it gave many years of excellent service, finally being scrapped on site in November 1970. Two more 4-wheeled diesel-mechanicals followed from Fowlers in 1949 and 1951 but these were Marshall engines on a 'Resilient' chassis and although they both lasted, one being sold on in 1974 and the other also scrapped on site in 1970, they were not popular with their drivers, as they rattled excessively.
[BERNARD ROBERTS COURTESY IRS]

A decade or so later, North Devon Clay took delivery of four Ruston 4-wheeled diesel mechanicals, two in 1959, one in 1961 and the last in 1965. The 1959-built locomotive, Works No. 435398, is seen here heading away to the clay pits with a selection of open wagons for loading on 16th September 1966. In 1972, it went to the Seaton & District Electric Tramway, where it was regauged to 2ft 9ins, but since 2002 has been at Devon Railway Centre, established at the old Cadeleigh station site.
[PHILIP HINDLEY]

The transshipment siding, where narrow gauge wagons filled with ball clay on the loading bank were emptied by hand into standard gauge wagons below. The pits are still being worked today but since 1982, when the branch from Barnstaple to Torrington finally closed, the clay has been entirely transported out by road.
[PHILIP HINDLEY]

4
A MISSED PRESERVATION OPPORTUNITY:
THE 3FT RAVENGLASS & ESKDALE RAILWAY

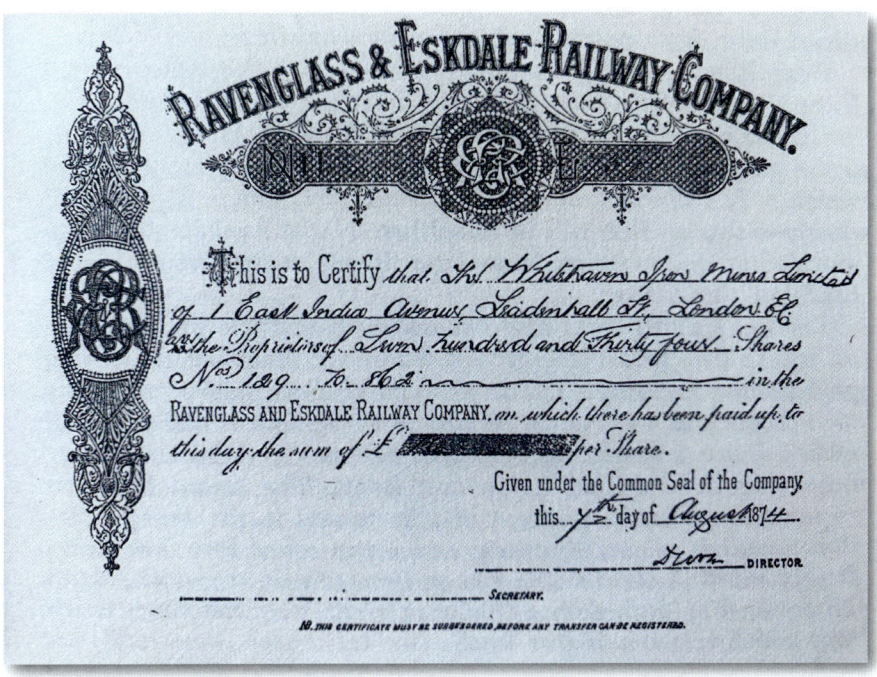

The roads are awe inspiring in their steepness, but there is a still more surprising railway. North of Barrow in Furness is a junction called Ravenglass. "Change here for the Eskdale line" calls the porter. As your ticket is for Irton Road on that line, you dismount and look around for your train. The porter collects your goods and, stepping across the rails past a goods shed, leads you to a tiny siding whereby is a tar coated wooden shed, covering some extremely crookedly laid rails, three feet in gauge. On the rails are an engine of primitive design, a van ditto, and one coach still more so. The coach is a "composite" one, containing a guard's box, one third "smoker" and an ordinary third. These carriages hold at a pinch four slim adults a side, and are innocent alike of racks, cushions or communication cords. As, however, the pace never exceeds five miles an hour, nervous passengers need not be deterred from journeying on the line on this account, for it is quite within the bounds of safety to alight while the train is going at full speed.

There are no porters visible, but presently a guard arrives, and the engine, which has been employing its leisure giving rides to two small boys, is coupled on ahead, and the guard, a composite official, unlocks a cupboard in the dim recesses of the shed and doles out four third class tickets to the three others and yourself who comprise his load. Then he locks up his "ticket office" and, packing you in, starts his tiny train on its perilous career up the valley. It lurches, and groans, and rolls along in a manner that makes you wonder why you did not invest your spare coppers in insurance tickets. You also speculate whether the bottom will fall out of the carriage, the train pull up the rails, or the whole affair topple over into the river.

Thick bracken brushes the footboards at either side, from out of which the head of an ancient Herdwick ram gazes up at the snorting, labouring engine. It is evidently an old acquaintance, and he pays but little heed to it. The stoker, whistling cheerfully, sits on the cab, swinging one leg over the side with an airy grace all his own. Presently with a dislocating jerk, the train pauses dead with an abruptness that lands your portmanteau on its toes, and the stoker descends leisurely to drive a misguided ewe and lamb off the track into the clustering bracken. This act of mercy being accomplished, and a pedestrian who suddenly appears over a wall having climbed aboard for a 'lift', this weird express grunts its toilsome way at last into "Irton Road Station", a wooden hut with a siding whereon reposes a decaying truck filled with bricks. Here you dismount, and the guard, who has unlocked the hut and doled out more tickets, starts his comic opera collection of relics off again on its uncertain way round a bend, up into the beautiful cleft among the hills where, several stations away, lies the terminus, which is known as Boot.

[Mary Fair, *Wide World* 19th December, 1903]

Two identical Manning, Wardle 0-6-0 side tank locomotives were ordered for the opening of the railway, with *Devon* arriving first at the end of May 1875, handling all the traffic until her sister, *Nab Gill*, arrived a year later. Livery in the early days was dark lined green with the name on the side tanks (together with the usual 'full stop' added in Victorian times) and the letters R&ER on the front buffer beam. Later, the locomotives may have been painted black but certainly lost their lining. In this picture a Lowca Engineering plate had been added to the running board after she was repaired there in the 1890s. Normally, both locomotives were maintained by fitters from the Furness Railway when needed and, on occasions, they were sent to the FR's Moor Row workshops when facilities at Ravenglass proved insufficient. [JOHN ALSOP COLLECTION]

A Missed Preservation Opportunity: The 3ft Ravenglass & Eskdale Railway

The main problem which restrained the development of the three foot gauge Ravenglass & Eskdale line was the lack of money to convert the railway to mainly a passenger carrying concern within a rapidly growing tourist paradise. Despite some efforts to raise the required capital to do this, the promoters were not successful, probably because the railway had followed a chequered career and few believed in an Eldorado.

But, imagine now the scene at Ravenglass station as it could have been, with tourists thronging the station waiting to board the heavily booked mid-morning train to Scafell View at the head of the Eskdale valley. A long train of identical 4-wheeled carriages painted brown but ornately lined out in gold stand by the platform ready for service. At the front of the train is a handsome large 6-coupled saddle tank steam locomotive painted light green built by Peckett of Bristol. The station is a simple but effective affair with a wooden overall roof and separate modern café and shop.

Passengers board and our train leaves, running slightly downhill alongside the River Esk with immediate views of the lake district mountains and even the famous Scafell Pike, England's highest mountain. Soon we leave the river valley, run past a mill and head through the woods with ever-changing scenery to Irton Road, the passing point for trains. The station is attractively set on a slight curve just below a farmhouse and some cottages reached by a delightful stone bridge across the railway in the middle of the station.

We continue our journey up through Eskdale Green, forest and farmland and find the last stretch of the journey to be highly exhilarating as our locomotive has to work much harder to climb the final half mile to the delightful village of Boot and its water mill.

Of course, a journey quite like this has never been possible. For some years, one could take a narrow gauge train on this exact journey, in wooden carriages hauled by a 6-coupled tank locomotive, but the railway was then designed to carry iron ore, not really for tourist passengers, although they were certainly carried. You can now make most of this journey by a 15 inch gauge miniature train which has built up a DNA all of its own. But what went wrong with the seemingly idyllic narrow gauge train?

The answer lies in the iron ore mineral extraction business and also in a very early attempt to 'preserve' the railway which served it when the mines failed.

In theory a railway built to carry iron ore from the mines to industry should have been successful for many years, just as those railways built in the rich strata of thick easily worked layers of ore found just under the surface in the limestone wolds of Northampton were. But the Ravenglass & Eskdale Railway struggled. The reason lies in the nature of the iron ore deposits in Cumbria. This ore is of a different type, haematite, which is found in folds and pockets of older granite rocks in the area. The disadvantage of this is that the ore deposits exist only in erratic veins, which often fade out almost without warning or are found only in isolated pockets. The ore is hard to win, yet in times of high demand may still be worth the considerable effort and expense. In western Cumberland, these deposits were within relatively easy reach of the iron and steel towns of Millom and Workington which grew up because of the presence of this haematite. Around 1870, the demand for iron ore temporarily rapidly increased due to the Franco-Prussian war. This encouraged entrepreneurs to look a bit further afield for more ore as it was known that the Romans had worked deposits in Eskdale and Miterdale with numerous lodes existing, particularly in the fell between the valleys.

So, the Whitehaven Iron Mines Limited was formed to exploit this opportunity, with sponsors attracted from far afield, including the Earl of Devon. They did a not particularly well-thought-out deal to buy the mining rights from an extremely canny character, Faithful Cookson, who most certainly saw them coming. In fact, he may well have obtained the best bargain of all: a sum of cash, no risk and the right to have the land back. The mines provided some initial successes but when the veins were exhausted, fortunes fell.

But the ore at Nab Gill was different and available in marketable quantities, despite being further away from civilisation and really too far for horse and cart traffic. So enters the Ravenglass & Eskdale Railway, promoted in 1872 as a separate concern to build a railway 'between 2ft 9 inches and standard gauge' to the Furness Railway at Ravenglass and even with powers to build to the harbour there, although this had been silted up for years. The line was actually built to three foot gauge and clearly intended to be only for the mineral traffic and was constructed accordingly and opened by May 1875, worked by two side tank 6-coupled steam locomotives built by Manning, Wardle. One took the name *Devon*, after the Earl who was one of the quarry founders, and the other *Nab Ghyll*, after the most marketable quarry. The quarry company took up half the share capital with the contractor building the line taking the other half. Lord Muncaster attended the opening on 20th November to give the 8.25am first train a formal send off by riding on the footplate all the way to Boot.

As there was only a single customer, the fortunes of the railway followed those of the mining company, who had entered the arena to recover not the easiest form of iron ore at a time of high demand, but which was short lived. So, historians are not surprised that its existence was troubled, to say the least. Within a year of opening, the railway found itself 'in Chancery', that is to say insolvent and managed by a receiver appointed by the court on behalf of creditors. The contractor was owed money which it could not pay and so sued for this with the expectation of being awarded possession of the physical plant (despite being a 50 per cent shareholder). The mining company was then obliged to petition the Chancery Court to stabilise the position so that the railway could at least carry on in some form.

In this situation, the receiver simply used any operating surplus to deal with maintenance, although he did use local resources to build more rolling stock, including another carriage.

After various ups and downs, and even a branch to Gill Force on the River Esk being built to work a new deposit, the inevitable happened and the mining company failed. Ordinarily, this would also have been the end of the railway but, as it was a separate concern, it was able to carry on as best it could carrying traffic from the remaining mines and on a 'make do and mend basis'. But, in the last years of the 19th century, traffic really only materialised from local goods and an increasing number of tourists who came to visit the beautiful Eskdale valley in the summer months. Even so, there were between three or four trains daily. Interestingly, it was probably

'What do you think of this one? Tuesday last we had our long promised day up the river. It was simply glorious weather & just a delightful breeze.' This charming commercial postcard (The Wrench Series No. 5508) with this wording written on the back shows *Nab Gill* with a train near Horsefalls, approximately three miles from Ravenglass, around 1904, steaming along in the beautiful scenery of the valley. Note there is no brake van on the train. The good condition of the track contrasts with later views. *Nab Gill* expired around 1904-5 but continued to exist donating parts to sister *Devon* when required, even though it ceased to be referred to in the various leases and other documents when the railway changed hands. [MICHAEL WHITEHOUSE COLLECTION]

Nab Gill coupled to the First Class carriage at Ravenglass. [JOHN ALSOP COLLECTION]

the case that if Chancery costs and debenture interest charges were excluded from the railway's costs, there might well have been enough operating surplus to do something more about maintaining the railway and converting it into a tourist line even then. But, in 1900, not many people were really seriously thinking about promoting quaint steam railways just for tourism. However, the August bank holiday trains in that year required both locomotives double heading to carry the traffic. But the Whitehaven News recorded that the prospects for the winter were not good.

However, on 16th November, 1907 a conscientious man named Edward Moore called a meeting at Carnforth and people were persuaded to support a scheme for rebuilding the railway to carry passengers. Rebuilding it certainly needed. Earnings for the previous two years had failed to cover expenses, the Nab Gill locomotive had expired, the wagon stock reduced to twenty serviceable vehicles, whilst the carriages were literally falling to pieces and the track was really unsafe for passenger carrying. But in the height of summer, even some of the mineral wagons had to be pressed into passenger service but still this did not provide enough rolling stock to meet the demand. Even these circumstances had not encouraged the management to advertise the beauty of Eskdale or encourage tourists to use the line.

Nevertheless the *Whitehaven News* of Thursday 23rd July, 1908 carried a prospectus addressed to those who are interested in the preservation of the railway and the development of the district of the Eskdale Valley, declaring that: '*so many people are concerned in the existence of the R&ER which is vital to the prosperity of the district... an estimate has been prepared for the necessary expenditure for the relaying of about four miles of track...to provide three new passenger carriages and an additional locomotive...repay the costs of the Chancery proceedings and to put an end there to, and thus enable the Company with a new Board of Directors to resume control.*'

It was probably the perfect answer and such a plan may well have enabled the 'Lal Ratty' to survive into the era of a growing tourist industry. Unfortunately, the hoped-for public support failed to materialise, probably because the railway had followed a chequered career to date and the prospectus had not been underwritten by any philanthropists or investors. Nevertheless, enough interest was generated from a few individuals to raise enough money to form the Eskdale Railway Company to acquire the undertaking of the R & ER by means of a new Act of Parliament. Whilst these proceedings were grinding away, fortunately the Eskdale Mining Company resuscitated itself enough to lease the railway and run a daily train, which kept the line alive.

The new railway company resolved to try to keep the railway running whilst they sought additional funds for repairs and improvements. The operation was still not a success as receipts failed to cover costs. But this was not quite yet the end, as the mining company still required the railway to move its ore and negotiated a lease to enable it to do so, with more leases of railway and mine sites being negotiated and a thrice weekly service recommenced from Easter in 1911. Although matters were said to be "going well" with the usual hopes for a full scale revival, the

A Phoenix series commercial postcard, with elements tinted, depicts *Devon* on the 'Express' at Eskdale Green around 1903. The station platform was then much closer to the road overbridge. By now the locomotive had been repaired by the Lowca Engineering Company, probably in 1898 when air braking equipment was added (handily for the identifier of photographs as the equipment was fitted to different sides of the two locomotives). Whilst the carriages already look rather battered and warped, the railway was offering a daily service of five trains to local people and visitors. [JOHN ALSOP COLLECTION]

Devon derailed at Murthwaite on 10th March 1905. By this time, the track had deteriorated causing this derailment to the 9.35am train up from Ravenglass. Whilst the position of the air compressor and the style of the smokebox door identify the locomotive as *Nab Gill*, the side tanks are carrying *Devon*'s name. Clearly parts were moved between locomotives most probably in order to keep at least one in service. [MICHAEL WHITEHOUSE COLLECTION]

Irton Road was the principle intermediate station on the railway and unique as it had the only stone built station building (which still exists in use today). This served the bobbin mill in Miterdale, the basket maker, the grocer and coal merchant at Eskdale Green as, before the days of the commercial lorry, the railway was a common carrier with everything into and out of the valley being transported by train. [JOHN ALSOP COLLECTION]

Two views of *Devon* with a heavily-loaded excursion train for Boot on Whit Monday 1906. The top picture shows the train arriving with the guard standing in the doorway of his coupé compartment in the Third Class carriage at the front of the train. The second view shows the train, comprising all of the carriages, the brake van and four mineral wagons, with everyone looking at the photographer, including the well-dressed lady climbing into the brake van. [MICHAEL WHITEHOUSE COLLECTION]

Devon hauling all the available rolling stock on, probably, another bank holiday train, approaching Irton Road. Clearly, the weather was a little more inclement on this occasion. Unlike most steeply graded railways, the 'Ratty' always ran both its locomotives facing down the prevailing gradients towards Ravenglass. [JOHN ALSOP COLLECTION]

Devon with a goods train, with the brake van in the middle, running back towards Ravenglass. The deteriorating trackwork and fencing are very evident. [MICHAEL WHITEHOUSE COLLECTION]

mines encountered shutdowns and flooding due to stormy weather and the mining company was always seemingly in financial difficulties, resulting in miners striking due to the skimping of safety precautions. On Monday 12th December, 1912, the miners arrived to find the lowest level of their mine flooded and water rising rapidly in the shaft. At this time, this was the only level being worked, as the mining company were "containing expenses" and, as there was no money to rectify the position, the mines finally closed. The railway staggered on through the winter, based purely on hope "things would recover," but they did not and so on 30th April, 1913, that was finally that.

The railway closed and lay moribund, remarkably to be rescued and transformed by 15 inch gauge miniature railway enthusiasts who procured enough funds to provide 'new' second-hand equipment. These enthusiasts secured a lease from the Chairman of the Eskdale Railway Company, Edward Bousefield Dawson. He had no personal authority to agree this without board approval and simply pocketed the proceeds. Most probably as being a creditor of the railway himself he saw this as the most practical way to recoup some of his losses. Dawson also sold the locomotives for scrap, the carriages to local farmers and had the wagons burned where they lay.

Devon taking water at Fisherground, at the foot of the incline to the Ban Garth mine. The water supply from this mine has never dried up and so the tank remains useable even today. [MICHAEL WHITEHOUSE collection]

Just think though, had that 1908 prospectus succeeded to create the concept of a 'preserved' tourist narrow gauge railway by sparking interest in investors at the time, L'al Ratty might just have been able to revitalise itself and carry enough summer passengers to survive. Perhaps if the railway had attracted the attention and political guile of Holman F. Stephens, enough local people or government authorities might have been convinced to part with rather more cash. Perhaps if the railway had the entrepreneurial board of directors who established the Rye & Camber Railway to enable them to play golf and townsfolk to visit the beach and had also managed to raise funds from residents in the various towns along the coast around the lake district, enough money could have been raised to rebuild the infrastructure, acquire more carriages and buy a third locomotive. The records show that the Ratty just about broke even carrying summer passengers even in its final ramshackle state and we all know the attraction of the lake district today. What a super 'repository' for the Padarn railway quarrymens' 4-wheeler carriages, suitably regauged. What opportunities there would have been to acquire many suitable three foot gauge steam locomotives from the Northamptonshire ironstone mine railway. And quite likely all for a 'song' in terms of purchase price. But we may dream.

Devon enters Ravenglass with a passenger train around 1905, over the bridge carrying the line across Main Street. Beyond the bridge parapet the locomotive shed can be seen, which is still in use today for the 15 inch gauge line. The substantial stone walls on the left were planned to support a high level siding, which would have enabled 3ft gauge wagons to unload into standard gauge ones below. As the railway went into receivership so quickly, it is uncertain whether this loading bank was ever completed. [MICHAEL WHITEHOUSE collection]

The 'Express' at Boot formed only of the Bristol Wagon Company-built carriages; one First and one Third Class. Despite trains being advertised in the time table as carrying First, Second and Third classes, no Second Class accommodation was ever provided. The First Class coach is behind the locomotive, followed by the Third Class coach with its coupé compartment for the guard, then by the brake van with 'birdcage' look out at the Ravenglass end. The Ravenglass-built 'big saloon' stands in the adjacent siding
[JOHN ALSOP COLLECTION]

When the railway was completed, there were initially many shortcomings requiring a second approval inspection. Station buildings were eventually provided, but not at Miteside where, even by 'Ratty' standards, the boat shelter was unusual. The old boat was placed there by Willie Salmon who lived in the large house amongst the trees beyond the river. The 15 inch gauge railway has copied this concept and installed a similar upturned boat section at its Miteside halt. [Michael Whitehouse collection]

Eskdale Green station with ladies and their dog on the platform/track. [Michael Whitehouse collection]

Holiday passenger train at Boot, again with all the available rolling stock. That the railway did not really provide for passengers is very evident in this picture with very limited station facilities and the mineral wagons being absolutely crammed with trippers. [JOHN ALSOP COLLECTION]

Beckfoot station around the turn of the century with the Stanley Ghyll Hotel on the left hand side, built in the 1890s. Nearby was Beckfoot Quarry which was operated sporadically in 3ft gauge days, but was later to provide the life blood for the railway from 1922 until 1953.
[MICHAEL WHITEHOUSE COLLECTION]

Well-to-do passengers board a train standing at Southwold station's single platform around 1910, having arrived from town and the local district by horse taxis. The station was an open one, without barriers, so all ticket checks were made on the train. Note the ornate electric light columns, the plentiful station seats and the handcart with a large wicker basket. [JOHN ALSOP COLLECTION]

5
SUFFOLK ENTERPRISE:
THE SOUTHWOLD RAILWAY

'Nowadays when there are so many schemes for light railways under discussion, those interested in them would do well to undertake a journey on the Southwold Railway. They will see much to interest them, apart from which fact they will find the air of Southwold singularly invigorating. The scenery along the line and around Southwold is exceptionally pretty. There are miles of land covered with a bright yellow gorse and several acres devoted to pine trees. In June, Southwold is particularly attractive, for wild flowers of many varieties are plentiful, and the air is heavy with the scent of honeysuckle. There is, therefore, small cause for wonder that the Directors of the Southwold Railway Company are enabled to say in their last half yearly report: "The accounts show a satisfactory increase from all sources of traffic." There is, however, cause for wonder in the next clause of the report: "The working expenses under maintenance are less; under other heads they are slightly increased, but the result is a less amount on gross total expended."'
[Scott Damant, *The Railway Magazine*, 1899]

This 'delightful little toy railway', connecting with the Great Eastern Railway at Halesworth and running 8 ¾ miles to the seaside resort town and harbour of Southwold, via Wenhaston, Blythburgh and Walberswick villages, carried close on 100,000 passengers annually in its heyday, with steadily increasing volumes of all types of traffic until defeated by the consequences of the Great War: Government control, increase in costs resulting in lack of maintenance and finally ousted by the motor bus. However, operating profitably for over forty years in more or less its original form should be heralded as a success.

Had Southwold not deteriorated as a port midway on the

Sharp, Stewart & Co agreed to supply three identical 2-4-0T locomotives with payment over seven years, No's 1-3 and named *Southwold*, *Halesworth* and *Blyth* respectively. The locomotives were used turn and turnabout with one working the 'one engine in steam' service, a second as standby and the third under maintenance. Originally, they were painted in the maker's mid-green livery, lined out in black, edged white, but after visits to the GER Stratford works in 1887, No's 2 & 3 returned in blue livery with red lining and probably red coupling rods. From around 1895 black livery prevailed. [Michael Whitehouse collection]

ABOVE: No. 2 *Halesworth* at Southwold on 11th August 1923. [A.W. CROUGHTON, MICHAEL WHITEHOUSE COLLECTION]
BELOW: No. 3 *Blyth* in the station yard at Southwold. [MICHAEL WHITEHOUSE COLLECTION]

Suffolk coast between Aldborough and Lowestoft and had the Great Eastern Railway played a weaker hand in the development discussions, it might perhaps have survived longer and even been converted to standard gauge. There were various schemes to improve the harbour by dredging resulting in calls to convert the SR to standard gauge and sell it to the GER, or its successor the LNER, but these all failed. The interests of Lowestoft and the GER maintaining its monopoly there largely saw to that, although the board of directors of the Southwold, chaired by Richard Rapier, of the well known Ipswich engineering firm and assisted by the extensive experience of Arthur Pain, civil engineer and managing director, were a competent team and managed their enterprise well.

The three foot gauge railway was opened in 1879, created, as usual in those times, by its own Act of Parliament. Well, easily and simply constructed and initially worked on a 'one engine in steam basis', the railway steadily grew its traffic to effect and paid annual dividends. Originally, three locomotives from Sharp, Stewart & Co. were ordered, but traffic needs only really dictated two initially, so one was handed back to the builder and ended up in Columbia of all places. Later, as the traffic grew, a new third locomotive was purchased and, in anticipation of a significant increase in traffic from Southwold harbour after reconstruction in 1914, a fourth larger and more modern locomotive was built.

The railway was simply but sufficiently appointed and equipped: six tramway style bogie coaches and several wagons (including from 1896 Cleminson 6-wheeled wagons built by private owner, Thomas Moy) together with delightful stations built from brick with timber framing, described as 'a happy combination of cheapness and convenience.'

Initially, the board of directors had their work cut out to establish the railway and develop the traffic. Arthur Pain pushed Southwold Corporation to develop housing and have the harbour dredged as it had further silted up and, initially, there was little prospect of a dividend. But as Richard Rapier commented at the 1886 employees' dinner *"they were making good progress and meeting working expenses"*, passenger numbers increased and likewise goods traffic receipts. The railway had to seek to survive and grow within the state of the national and local economies as these fluctuated. Bad weather, a trade depression and then an unusually poor fishing season in 1886 initially did not help. But these were temporary setbacks for, by 1888, Arthur Pain was able to tell the staff at their annual December dinner in the Southwold Town Hall that the decline in passenger traffic had been arrested and parcels, goods and mineral traffic had shown a marked increase. The railway was on the up and successfully raised a further £12,000 worth of capital by a debenture issue in the following year. In 1893, the staff praised the 'brilliant leadership' of Richard Rapier and added that visitors to the town always spoke in the highest terms of the civility of the company's servants.

The board continued to improve the commercial operation of the railway whilst battling with the Board of Trade against the need to fit continuous brakes, continuing to encourage Southwold Corporation to dredge the harbour so it could be kept open for sea traffic and perhaps developed. It also began to engage with Governmental authorities and connecting railways to discuss the practicality of either sale to the Great Eastern Railway or conversion to standard gauge; even an arrangement with the new Mid Norfolk railway was discussed to provide an alternative route to Lowestoft, but there was never really enough business to justify that, and the GER was certainly not keen to entertain a local competitor.

Meantime, each half yearly report turned in good results, showing increases in all traffic, a surplus of income over expenditure and an ability to pay dividends. On bank holiday, 2nd August 1897 the trains were packed with passengers seeking to spend a few hours by the sea at Southwold; brilliant sunshine and cloudless skies resulted in the crowds staying as long as they could in the town, so that the 7.15pm departure hauled by No. 1 *Southwold* was formed of six very full carriages. The summer season had been the best yet with hundreds of tourists demanding accommodation. Passengers travelling neared 100,000, with 31,161 tons of parcels, 5,346 tons of goods traffic and 6,664 tons of mineral traffic carried. Once again, the fishing industry turned to look at what could be done to improve Southwold harbour as the herring fishing industry at both Yarmouth and Lowestoft was now extremely prosperous and more facilities were needed.

All this encouraged more discussions about obtaining a Light Railway Order to upgrade the railway to standard gauge, extend it and provide for the Great Eastern to work it. Various reports, surveys and proposals to bring all these modernisations were prepared and discussed at length for, as Alderman Adnams of Southwold Town Council aptly commented: *"the railway had arrived in the district when badly wanted, had been of great assistance and helped the town to expand, but now the time had come for a better service, more direct communication with London and to obviate the transhipment of goods."* Laudable objectives, but never actually to be achieved on the Southwold Railway, although its board did actually start work on bridge widening including rebuilding the swing bridge by the harbour.

By 1907, progress was made with the Southwold harbour scheme by dredging, which encouraged the directors of the GER to visit. But they took the view that the size of the harbour, the depth of water and width of its entrance would still only be suitable for fishing boats and small traders and so would not be any threat to the prosperity of Lowestoft. Of course, this result suited them, but they still came to look. The GER also expressed concern that the SR was asking the Light Railway Commissioners for permission to convert to standard gauge as this was not at all in their interests, although it was of course content to have the SR as a feeder. However, a contractor, Fasey & Company, had secured a Government grant of £21,000 (about a quarter of the cost) to deepen the harbour, extend old piers and build a new fish market, which led to a Scottish syndicate owning 400 herring drifters being tempted to Southwold. Faseys also bought the harbour from the Council and even offered to build a branch to the harbour for the SR. Perhaps enticed by all this, the railway company issued more debenture stock and installed a passing loop at Blythburgh.

The railway was still making a profit, sufficient to pay debenture interest at 4-5 per cent. Furthermore, by 1909, the board announced the lowest recorded percentage of working expenses to gross receipts and applied to the Treasury for a grant to widen the line to standard gauge. It also tempted the GER to get involved again to construct the standard gauge line and harbour extension and provide rolling stock in return for

Wenhaston, a 0-6-2T, was delivered from Manning, Wardle in July 1914, following a request for a locomotive which could haul heavy loads. She was painted in dark green livery, lined out in light and dark green. She is seen here at Halesworth in April 1929.
[MICHAEL WHITEHOUSE COLLECTION]

debentures, but this was not agreed. Fasey even wanted the GER to buy the SR out completely. Hyde, the GER General Manager, was of the opinion that it would cost his railway £100,000 to bring the SR up to scratch and convert it to standard gauge and considered the prospect 'unremunerative to his company'. His view was probably coloured for, when he visited Southwold harbour, all he saw was coal being discharged from two sailing colliers and most fish landed being exported again by sea, neither 'touching the railway'.

Meanwhile, still making a profit with increasing traffic, the railway obtained a Light Railway Order to build the harbour branch and, in 1914, ordered a new more powerful locomotive from Manning, Wardle, an 0-6-2T named *Wenhaston*, in anticipation of increased traffic. The prospects looked good.

However, as so often happens to the best laid plans, something comes in from left field to throw them into array. In 1914, of course, this was the outbreak of First World War. Whilst this initially had little impact, the duration and assumption of control by the Government was to be the first nail in the coffin for development and indeed existence. Coupled with this, visits by holidaymakers were of course drastically reduced as the district was considered a likely area for German invasion. However, the railway managed to cope with all the military requirements in moving troops, food and munitions, so still made a profit and

Ten years after returning No. 1 *Southwold* to the manufacturer due to perceived lack of demand, the railway realised it did need three steam engines and so, in 1893, ordered a new one, a 2-4-2T this time, also from Sharp, Stewart which assumed No. 1's name. This is the manufacturer's works photo with No. 1 in the usual photographic grey livery, lined in black with double white edging, chosen so as to bring out all the features of the design best on black & white glass negatives. [JOHN ALSOP COLLECTION]

Southwold station forecourt in the early years, probably 1898, showing the station building as originally built. No. 3 *Blyth* stands in the station with a short train comprising a van and two carriages, both in a cream livery with black panelled lining. There is a third coach in the siding beyond the locomotive in the original maroon livery. This seems almost certainly a publicity shot taken around 1890 when two carriages were repainted in the lighter colour and posed to show off their new livery. Of course, this was a difficult livery to keep clean and so, by around, 1919 they began to revert to maroon. [JOHN ALSOP COLLECTION]

The Southwold Railway

A postcard sent in 1903 showing the railway near Eastwoodlodge Farm at the western end of Walberswick Common looking towards Halesworth. The railway employed two permanent way gangs to maintain the entire line and fencing and, in this view, everything is neatly in place. As trains never ran very fast, often also with several stops for shunting and also waiting time waiting connections at Halesworth, journey times were not very fast, hence the comment on the reverse of the card that it took three hours to get to Lowestoft. [John Alsop collection]

The 'Southwold Express' leaves the town's station around 1904 for a posed publicity shot. Three well dressed children stand on the fence waving to a lady, possibly their mother, who waves back from the balcony of the second carriage. Normally passengers would not be allowed to remain on the balcony once the train was in motion. The open-sided carriage shed in the station siding constructed in 1904 can clearly be seen, as can the new Station Hotel. This view was published in the well known Valentine's postcard series. [Neil Parkhouse collection]

Walberswick station in the 1890s (7 miles 46 chains from Halesworth) comprised a basic platform with simple wooden shelter. Two passengers await a train and several boxes labelled Thompson & Stroud are ready to be loaded on board. The picture is almost certainly posed as the men are looking in the wrong direction for the expected train, going by the signal arm lowered for its arrival. [John Alsop collection]

A tinted postcard published around 1905, showing the second No. 1 *Southwold* 2-4-2T waiting to leave Southwold bunker first, showing her in the early green livery during a winter's day as most of the staff are wearing coats. Locomotives were occasionally turned on their return from attention at the GER's Stratford Works in order to even out wheel tyre and flange wear. [John Alsop collection]

No. 3 *Blyth* stands at Southwold station with a mixed train in 1906. Wagons were always marshalled at the front of the train to simplify shunting en route. [JOHN ALSOP COLLECTION]

Close up of the somersault signal, point levers and rodding at the entrance to Southwold station; all interlocked by rodding. Note the spectacle glasses two thirds the way up the post and the lamp near the foot. [MICHAEL WHITEHOUSE COLLECTION]

The guard checks tickets inside one of the Third Class carriages. Pinned to the end wall are several posters advertising London connections by the L&NER.
[MICHAEL WHITEHOUSE COLLECTION]

paid dividends, but the war enforced abandonment of the aspirations to extend the line and convert it to standard gauge. Whilst the rolling stock had been in continual use for military requirements, this was without adequate maintenance and the equipment was also now becoming antiquated. Furthermore, running expenses increased with wages increasing from £1,300 to over £5,000 pa. By 1924 dividends ceased on account of rising costs caused by the war and the onset of road competition by motor bus. On top of all this, in 1926 there was a serious fatal accident whilst shunting at Wenhaston.

In the summer of 1928, the Southwold Council authorised the Eastern Counties Road Car Company to pick up passengers by bus within the town's boundary. This was further bad news for the railway, whose passenger traffic was decreasing at a fast rate now. The antiquated train being really no match for the modern buses. Three of the steam locomotives were aged and required replacement, the carriages were life expired, nearly all the goods wagons required refurbishing and the permanent was now poorly maintained. Wages were reduced and the directors admitted that the financial position was 'causing considerable anxiety'.

The railway could no longer stay open without financial assistance and, as none was forthcoming, the railway closed on 11th April 1929. The last trains, of course, were heavily loaded with well wishers, but at 5.23pm the last up passenger train departed Southwold behind Wenhaston and, apart from a few freight positioning trips, that was that. The railway was literally put out to grass. Amazingly the company itself continued to exist until 1994 before it was actually dissolved by administrators.

The Southwold Railway had a good run for its money. It had operated largely as built for some forty years, served its purpose well but had been run out of steam by a combination of war, increased costs, resolute competition and the arrival of the motor bus. As Southwold had a lesser harbour than Lowestoft, which would always give the GER better returns, this denied any prospect of the main line saving the narrow gauge by takeover. Compared with many other English narrow gauge common carrier railways though, the Southwold was successful: it served its purpose and made money until it became out of date.

Almost certainly a posed shot for an F. Jenkins publicity postcard. Frederick Jenkins had a thriving photographic processing, framing and general souvenir business which he ran from 94 High Street in Southwold. He was to become a significant figure for the town, being responsible for many of the images which have subsequently provided an important source to show what early 20th century life was like. In around 1906, with summer shadows falling from the chestnut tree, No. 3 *Blyth* stands surrounded by the train crew, station staff, several fruit baskets and a large passenger trunk. The locomotive has a large sand box atop its water tank and the usual oil can sits on the footplate. [MICHAEL WHITEHOUSE COLLECTION]

No. 1 *Southwold* arrives at Halesworth station with an evening mixed train around 1910. There was no room for a run round loop within station limits so this had to run at the back of the station building. A porter is ready to collect the single line token from the locomotive crew and another to assist passengers from the train; where are all the porters now? [JOHN ALSOP COLLECTION]

Southwold station with No. 3 *Blyth* in the run round loop shortly before the First World War. The engine shed is in the background to the left and the goods shed and loading platform stand to the right of it, facing the platform line headshunt. The station building had now been extended and behind it the hotel had been built. [JOHN ALSOP COLLECTION]

The second *Southwold*, 2-4-2T No.1, stands in the station of its own name, preparing to run bunker first to Halesworth with a mixed train. Several of the wagons can again be seen quite clearly showing a tarpaulin-covered 4-wheeler, 6-wheeled open No. 28 and then two further 4-wheeled wagons. [MICHAEL WHITEHOUSE COLLECTION]

No. 3 *Blyth* shunts wagons in the yard at Southwold, with driver John Stannard in charge of her. The first wagon is a 6-wheeled Cleminson design with SR tarpaulin sheets covering its heavy load. No. 3 is now in 'GER style' unlined blue. On the extreme right of the picture stands Fitzhugh, the stationmaster, watching the antics of the photographer. [MICHAEL WHITEHOUSE COLLECTION]

Southwold station staff on the platform, next to one of the Third Class carriages (probably either No's 1 or 4), just before the withdrawal of passenger services in 1929. In earlier days the station master would have been called Hayward, being one of my maternal grandmother's relatives when the family was based at Saxmundham. However, in this picture the station master, Bert Girling, is the third from left with George Burley, guard, at the extreme left, then, to the right of Girling, Aldis (porter) and Self (drayman). Behind them are three further men: Marchant (General Post Office clerk), Fisk (locomotive driver) and A. Barratt Jenkins who documented the line in its later years. [MICHAEL WHITEHOUSE COLLECTION]

Several narrow gauge railways were pilloried in local postcards and the SR did not escape. Here are a set of six amusing cartoons from the 'Sorrows of Southwold' series No. 2, drawn and published by Reg Carter of Southwold in 1910. The printed note on the reverse says 'With apologies to all'.
[DAVE WALDREN COLLECTION]

THE SOUTHWOLD EXPRESS: THE DRIVER DOES A ROARING TRADE OWING TO A DELAY CAUSED BY THE PORTER-OVERESTIMATING HIS STRENGTH - THE GUARD MAKES THE MOST OF THIS, AND TRIES

THE SOUTHWOLD EXPRESS - THE GUARD AS A PROFITABLE SIDELINE - PUTS THE DINNERS OF THE COTTAGERS ALONG THE ROUTE ON THE UP TRAIN - THESE BEING DONE TO PERFECTION BY THE RETURN JOURNEY - THE PROCESS OF CURING THE RENOWNED SOUTHWOLD BLOATERS IS SHEWN

THE SOUTHWOLD EXPRESS THE FIRST CLASS PASSENGER SUPPORTED BY ALL THE THIRD CLASS, SHEW GREAT ANNOYANCE AT AN UNEXPECTED STOP - TO LEARN FROM THE GUARD, THAT "THE DRIVER SEEING A CHOICE CROP OF GROUNDSEL - IS GATHERING IT FOR HIS CANARY!"

THE SOUTHWOLD EXPRESS :—
THE GOODS TRAIN LEAVES HALESWORTH HALF AN HOUR TOO SOON - THUS MEETING THE 2.20. FROM SOUTHWOLD BETWEEN BLYTHBURGH AND WENHASTON - AFTER MUCH DISCUSSION THE DRIVERS DECIDE TO FIGHT FOR THE RIGHT OF THE ROAD - A SPORTING PASSENGER MAKES THE MOST OF THE SITUATION - THE GUARD WAITS ANXIOUSLY

THE SOUTHWOLD EXPRESS - A HEAVY RAIN PUTS THE FIRE OUT - THE DRIVER FIXES A PASSENGERS' UMBRELLA - THE FIREMAN LIGHTS THE FIRE - THE GUARD DISREGARDFUL OF OF THE WEATHER BRAVELY SUPERINTENDS THE WHOLE UNPLEASANT OCCURRENCE.

THE SOUTHWOLD EXPRESS A COW ON THE LINE IS LUCKILY SEEN BY THE GUARD - IN HIS EAGERNESS TO STOP THE TRAIN HE PUTS THE BRAKES ON TOO SUDDENLY !

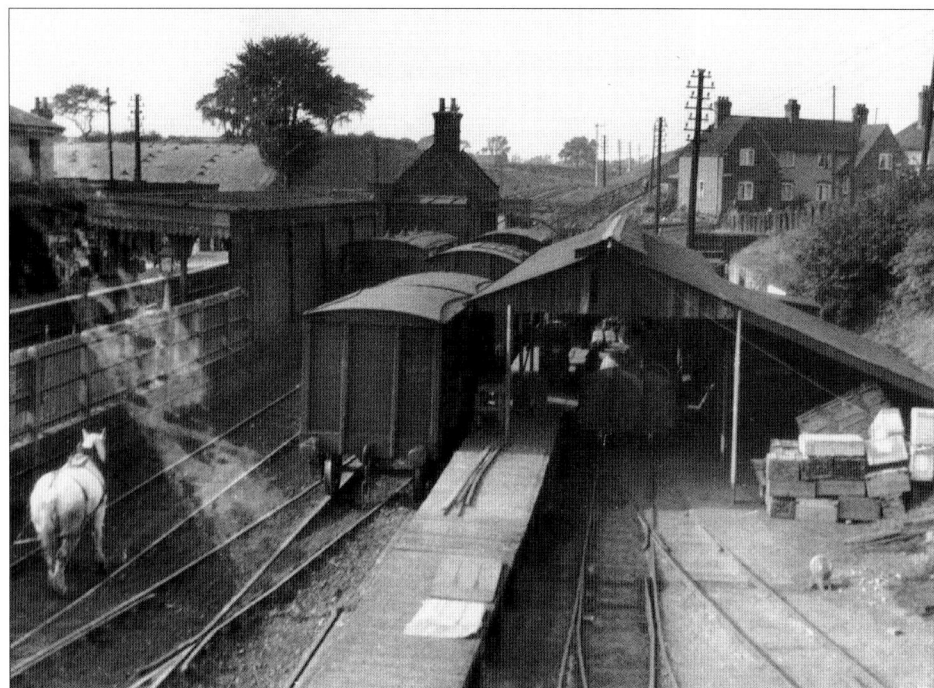

Halesworth exchange goods yard, sometime before 1929. Narrow gauge wagons are inside the transit shed adjacent to the standard gauge yard which is still then being shunted by horse.
[MICHAEL WHITEHOUSE COLLECTION]

T. Moy & Sons provided several of its own coal wagons to run on the SR. They were built to Cleminson's design: 6-wheeled with the centre wheel flexible to enable sharper curves to be negotiated. These wagons were painted in red oxide with black underframes. Here is No. 1511 seen at Halesworth on 3rd August 1931. Some of these wagons were later sold to the SR for its own use.
[JOHN ALSOP COLLECTION]

In 1936, three well known enthusiasts, John Adams and brothers Peter and Jim Jarvis visited the SR to photograph the locomotives then still in store, although the railway had been closed since 1929. With some difficulty they managed to pinch bar No. 3 *Blyth* out of Halesworth shed, cleaned her up and took several photographs. Jim recalled that he was the youngest of the three at the time but still used up to six glass plates in a day for photography.
[JOHN ADAMS]

6
REMUNERATIVE RAILWAYS FOR NEW COUNTRIES:
RANSOMES & RAPIER LTD

[Extracted and abridged from Richard Rapier's *Remunerative Railways for New Countries*, published in 1878]

'There is always considerable unwillingness to deviate from established types, and the desire to have as big and good railways as anyone else, has led many into extravagance and mischief, both in this and other countries.'
[Richard Rapier, 1878]

Folklore has it that the first train on the Southwold Railway ran through the meadows decorated with green dragons, being one of a pair ordered by the Emperor of China and not delivered because the devil was supposed to be within the first one. Legend also has it that the rails of this railway were actually second hand, retrieved from the Yangtze river in China and that the wooden balconied carriages running on the line were originally intended for the Woosung Railway, near Shanghai. It is even recorded that the first engineer on the Southwold Railway, W.G. Jackson, also drove the last train on the Woosung Railway.

There almost certainly is not much, if any, truth in this, although just maybe the Southwold carriages, built by the Bristol Tramway & Carriage Company, were part of a cancelled order originally intended for an extension of the Woosung Railway from Kangwan.

What do these railways have in common? The answer is Richard Rapier whom we met in the last essay when he was Chairman of the Southwold Railway. Before this railway was created, this entrepreneur was already in business promoting remunerative railways, although his Ipswich firm was probably better known in its latter days for the construction of massive walking dragline excavators. Ransomes & Rapier built some twenty-two steam engines for export to China, India, Hawaii and Malaya. His concept was undoubtedly sound and, indeed, some enterprises followed his wise words, at least indirectly, but his firm was not to become one of the significant exporters of steam locomotives. Whilst Ransomes & Rapier did supply the first locomotive to run in Malaysia, they were eclipsed by much larger manufacturer, Hunslet, who we will meet shortly.

Richard Rapier himself explains his concept and describes his journey into railway manufacturing in Suffolk in his fascinating book *Remunerative Railways for New Countries* published in 1878. Rapier grasps the nettle of why narrow gauge light railways rarely worked economically and this is worth considering in the light of the discussions in the various essays in this book about the life and times, hopes and frustrations of the promoters of English narrow gauge railways. Rapier is right up front from the start.

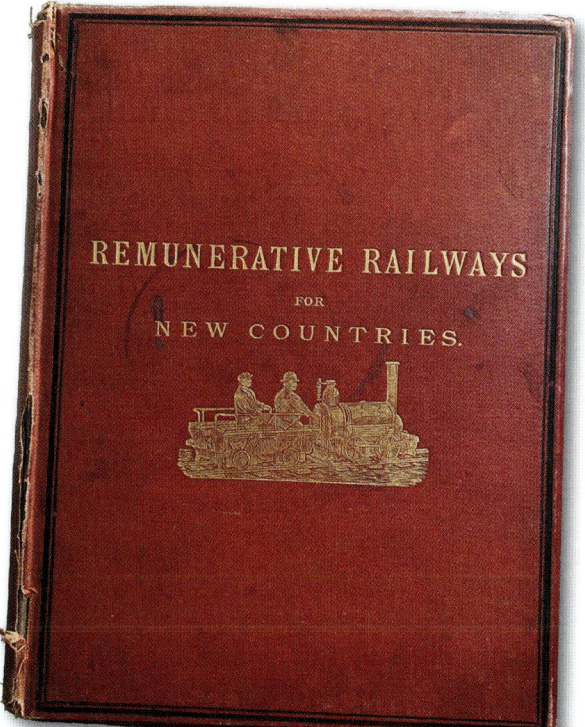

Remunerative Railways for New Countries written by Richard Rapier, Chairman of Ransomes & Rapier, in 1878, a hand backed volume, covered in red cloth with the title embossed in gold leaf; additionally, the pages were treated with gold leaf on their edges
[MICHAEL WHITEHOUSE COLLECTION]

'There is a general outcry, on the one hand, for more railways; and, on the other hand, that many of the lines already made do not pay their way satisfactorily. The following pages have been written, in the hope of contributing somewhat towards a remedy; at any rate as regards future undertakings.

The practice of relying on guarantees, for the interest on capital, has to answer for much of the present stagnation and difficulty in introducing new works. In proposed railways abroad, it has only been too common, for a State to be asked to guarantee a dividend, upon as large a capital as the authorities

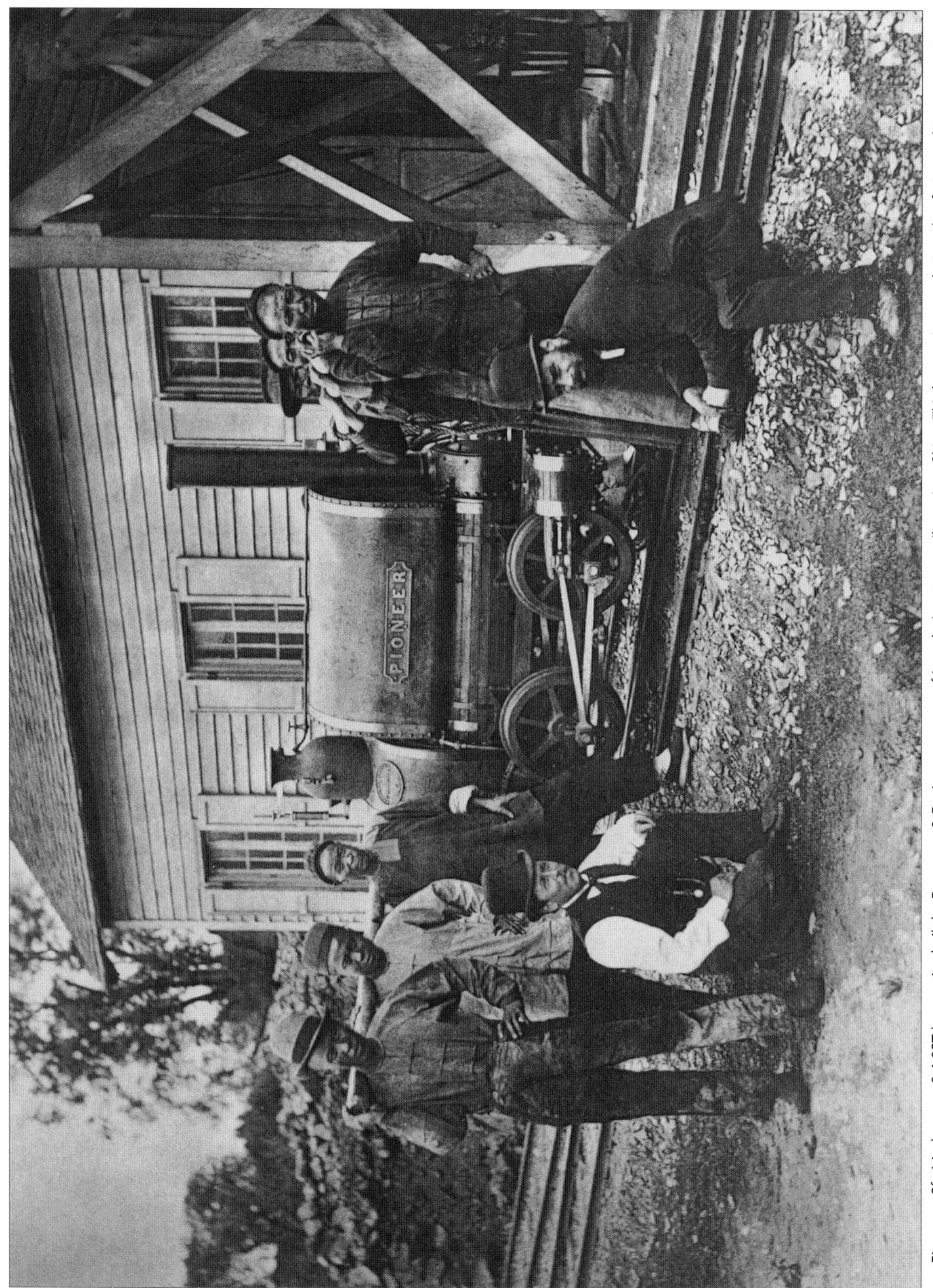

Pioneer, a 2ft 6 inch gauge 0-4-0ST locomotive built by Ransomes & Rapier as a means of introducing steam railways into China. This locomotive was designed to fit into a shipping case in one piece and work literally 'straight out of the box'. [MICHAEL WHITEHOUSE COLLECTION]

Engraving from a contemporary photograph taken by W. Sanders of Shanghai and reproduced in the *Illustrated London News* of 2nd September 1867, showing the official opening train of the Woosung Railway leaving Shanghai goods platform on 30th June 1876, headed by Rapier's 2ft 6 inch gauge 0-6-0T *Celestial Empire*. Another of the same class was named *Flowery Land*.

could be induced to sanction. Large capital powers, fortified by a Government guarantee, are pretty sure to be exercised; and thus, in many cases, the expenditure has been quite out of proportion to the needs of the locality. As a natural consequence, the earnings of such railways have not been equal to the guarantee; and States, like individuals, soon become tired of guarantees when they are called upon to pay them.

It seems probably that the next stage of railway development, throughout the world, will have to depend on the intrinsic merits of the undertakings, and their prospects of being able to earn their own living, rather than on any artificial support. It is therefore particularly opportune to inquire as to the practicability of introducing cheaper railways.

There is always considerable unwillingness to deviate from established types, and the desire to have as big and good railways as anyone else, has led many into extravagance and mischief, both in this and other countries.

During the last few years, much has been done towards facilitating the introduction of railways in the Colonies, and other distant countries, at greatly reduced cost as compared with the earlier railways. Not only has experience brought about the natural result of improved production, but a new departure altogether has been taken in constructing railways of a lighter calibre, than was formerly deemed practicable.

For the speeds required on our main lines in Great Britain, the ordinary gauge of 4ft 8 $\frac{1}{2}$ inches, with 80lb rail, maybe considered as the least which can be expected to discharge the required duty with safety and certainty. There are, however, many parts of England still in need of railway communication, which are not at all likely to demand any speed higher than 20 to 25 miles an hour.

For such localities much may be done by making the railways about half the ordinary size; the word 'size' is used because mere alteration of gauge will not make much difference – reduction to be of real use must be made throughout, especially in the weight of moving loads and in speed.

In the country the value of land is always a serious element in railway construction; and although there is no practical diminution in the quantity of land necessary for a narrow gauge railway, as compared with an ordinary one, the sharper curves which are practicable, enable considerable saving to be effected, by laying out the line so as to avoid severance as much as possible, and by selecting the least expensive route, both as regards value of land and cost of works.

Ransomes & Rapier's two 0-6-0Ts, *Flowery Land* and *Celestial Empire* pose for the photographer at the Woosung Railway's Shangai locomotive depot, together with a mix of English and Chinese staff. Richard Rapier must have been immensely proud of his railway, created out of packing cases shipped from his Suffolk works. The concept was backed by very many eminent British enthusiastic railway developers and promoted by Jardine Matheson, who were pre-eminent in Eastern business development, but the railway did not win favour with the Chinese and it was ripped up and destroyed. However, despite this setback, other British companies later succeeded in helping to create a railway system in this mysterious country. Sometimes the pioneers do not succeed and success is left to others who follow. [MICHAEL WHITEHOUSE COLLECTION]

Estimate of Materials and Fittings

FOR

TWENTY MILES OF RAILWAY FOR GENERAL TRAFFIC,

WITH

THREE INTERMEDIATE AND TWO TERMINAL STATIONS.

DUTY REQUIRED TO BE DONE.

1. Maximum train load required to be taken at 10 miles an hour on a level = 160 tons.
2. ,, ,, ,, ,, 7 ,, ,, up 1 in 100 = 75 ,,
3. ,, ,, ,, ,, 4 ,, ,, ,, 1 in 35 = 45 ,,
4. Speed with light loads = 22 miles an hour.

GAUGE, 2 ft. 6 in. to 3 ft. 6 in.

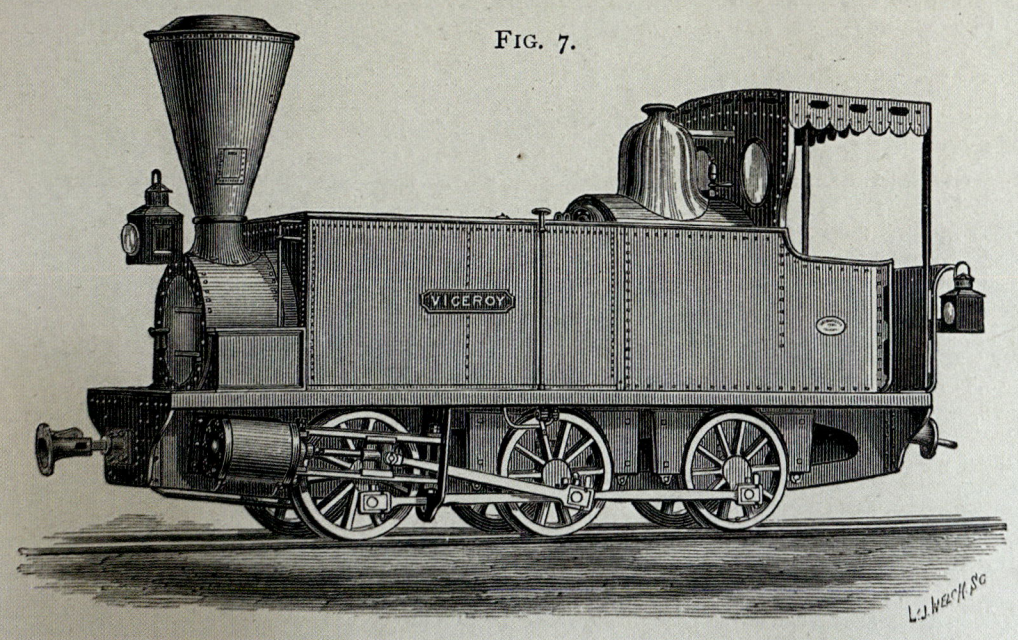

FIG. 7.

DESCRIPTION OF ENGINE SUITABLE FOR THE REQUIREMENTS.

1. Weight in working order, 12 tons, on 6 wheels, 2 ft. 6 in. diameter, all coupled.
2. Cylinders 9 in. × 14 in. Heating surface, 300 square feet. Grate area, 5 square feet.
3. Greatest weight on any wheel, 2 tons. Rails, 30 lbs. per yard. Gauge, 2 ft. 6 in. to 3 ft. 6 in.
4. Fixed wheel-base of Engines when made with six wheels coupled, 9 ft. 6 in.
5. Fixed wheel-base of Engines when made with four wheels coupled, and a "bogie," 5 ft. 0 in.

Ransomes & Rapier's advertisement for a standard narrow gauge 0-6-0T for 2ft 6 inch gauge with 8 $\frac{1}{2}$ inch x 12 inch cylinders and weighing 11 $\frac{1}{2}$ tons. It was built for the Shanghai-Woosung Railway in 1877 to Order No. 881, but had a remarkably short working life of only one month before the railway's closure, some would say prematurely. However, the Chinese who ordered its demise declared that it should never have been built, as they considered the concession to build was for a road, not a railway. Named *Viceroy*, it was the seventh steam locomotive built by the firm. [MICHAEL WHITEHOUSE COLLECTION]

However, Rapier's concept was sound and successfully adopted by one very determined British entrepreneur in Africa: Cecil Rhodes. In the last decade of the 19th century, Rhodes ordered the construction of the 2ft gauge Beira Railway in Mozambique, built with light rail at 20lbs per yard and small 4-4-0 locomotives to a standard design, all made by the Falcon Engine & Car Works of Loughborough. This enabled Rhodes' British South Africa Company to open up the African interior for development quickly and speed up the creation of the new Rhodesia as a corporately run country. The railway was built from the Portuguese port of Beira on the Indian Ocean. Largely simply laid on the ground, after hacking through jungle, and with several switchbacks, it reached the town of Umtali, just inside the new Rhodesian border, although the town had to be moved to the rail head due to the lie of the land. Within a couple of years from completion, growth in traffic carried by this 230-mile-long 2ft gauge railway required the line to be upgraded to the then standard 3ft 6 inch 'Cape gauge' adopted in Sub-Saharan Africa. It then formed an integral part of the network of Rhodesia Railways, which operated in both Northern and Southern Rhodesia, Mozambique and Botswana. This development followed almost precisely the concepts outlined by Rapier. Here, four of the Falcon 4-4-0s are seen on shed at Mandegos, the half way point, in 1899. When the line was upgraded, many of the locomotives found new lives on other industrial railways and even the locomotive shed was recycled as part of the Victoria Falls Hotel! [R.A.H. Baxter collection]

A light narrow gauge line can be made at a saving of £3,000 to £4,000 per mile, as compared with the cost of the cheapest ordinary line, and when it is borne in mind that every thousand pounds per mile of cost requires £1 per mile per week of net revenue to pay 5% dividend, the importance of every saving is very striking; and when it is further taken into account that a light railway, with small trucks and engines, can be maintained and worked more cheaply than a full sized line, a comparison is soon arrived at.

In all cases where there are no special circumstances suggesting a gauge of 2ft 6 inches or less, it would be advisable to adopt three feet as standard, because it admits of more commodious vehicles than the narrower gauge does, and if in the course of time a higher speed be demanded it can be obtained by gradually increasing the power of the engines and the weight of the rails as they are from time to time renewed. Railways still smaller have done excellent service, for what may be called private use as distinct from public traffic. At Woolwich Arsenal and at the Crewe Works of the London & North Western Railway, lines of 18 inch gauge are laid throughout the works for the conveyance of materials of all kinds with the aid of little locomotives built for the purpose. These lines have been in use for some years and are now indispensable. Their very narrow gauge, and the short wheelbase of the vehicles in use, enable curves of 20ft radius to be used, and thus the little railway penetrates into every corner of the premises.

It is often argued that a little railway may be all very well for a light traffic, but what is to be done when the traffic increases? To this it may be replied, that one of the greatest blunders has been making railways with too great a regard for the future, and not sufficient consideration for the immediate present. No business can stand a capital outlay which is out of proportion to the business to be done. It is familiar to all, that the successful manufactories and trading enterprises of this country have been the result of small first outlay, and gradual development of business. The man of business who begins in a small way keeps his premises and capital fully occupied, and success is the outcome of demand exceeding the supply.

In some of our colonies full sized railways have been made with the effect that the beginning of dividend paying is still distant; in others, railways have been made on a reduced scale of 3ft 6 inches gauge and 45lbs per yard; and in many of these, reports are to the effect that the railways do not pay for themselves, but they contribute to the prosperity of the country, and the public revenue is able to pay the guaranteed interest. Of course, where the country is able to bear it, this is all very well, and no very great harm may result in a growing country from making railways too expensive to be self supporting. But in the majority of cases it is a first necessity that the railways should pay as such; and the author has specially in view cases where no Government guarantee is obtainable; and in such instances the size of the railway to be made should be brought down to the level of the probable remuneration forthcoming at an early date.

In very many countries abroad the soil is literally teeming with valuable products; sometimes there is a great trading wealth in ivory, skins or other valuables. The difficulty of reaching the coast or a navigable river is usually the barrier to the general prosperity of the population. In such cases the smallest railway quickly executed would be an incalculable boon; and when the products are valuable and of moderate weight, the smaller the railway and the less the expenditure upon it, the better will be the results for all concerned.

The writer has been very much assisted by the incidental circumstances of his having for many years taken an active interest in the introduction of railways into China. That subject resolved itself into a question of the smallest practicable locomotive, which might be sent to that country in the most unobtrusive and inoffensive manner. In the result a little engine, named Pioneer, was made weighing only 30 cwt in working order, and capable of travelling 15 miles an hour (sometimes 20 miles) and able to draw two or three trucks of ballast each three times its own weight.

In 1865, a company was proposed for constructing a railway from Shanghai to Woosung, with a jetty and bonded warehouses at the latter place, by which the necessity for the passage of the larger class of steamers, up the difficult and changeable navigation to Shanghai could be avoided. Jardine, Matheson & Co gave cordial support, the Duke of Sutherland kindly lent his powerful aid to obtain for it a good hearing. The King of the Belgians also took a most lively interest in the proposal. British and Western statesmen warmly supported the proposal, and there seemed to be no doubt as to adequate funds being forthcoming, subscriptions being freely promised by manufacturing firms and others. The chief idea was to increase commerce between China and Britain.

A gauge of 2ft 6 inches was adopted for reasons of policy and economy. This opportunity has, however, abundantly proved the capabilities of such lines for good practical work in new countries.

The 9 ton Celestial Empire class have been constantly taking 200 to 250 passengers at a time, at a speed of 18 mile an hour. In a large majority if instances such a number of passengers to be conveyed at one time is quite outside of any immediate requirements in new countries, and to make any larger provision is simply to try to prevent the railway paying.

It is much to be regretted that the scheme was impracticable.'

This final sentence by Richard Rapier was a typical English understatement. The Woosung Railway was beset with problems from the start. The Chinese insisted that the concession granted to Jardine, Matheson had been for the construction of a road, not a railway, the *Pioneer* was unfortunately involved in a fatal accident which resulted in riots and the driver being tried for manslaughter. The railway was closed down and a temple dedicated to the Queen of Heaven erected on the site of its Shanghai terminus.

The opening day on 4th August 1883. Magnus Volk stands on the left-hand platform of the first car wearing a peaked cap lettered 'Volk's Electric Railway'. Mayor Cox takes up all the space on the right-hand platform. [BRIGHTON REFERENCE LIBRARY COLLECTON]

7
THE OLDEST ELECTRIC RAILWAY IN THE WORLD:
THE VOLKS ELECTRIC RAILWAY

As a physician I can conceive of no more advantageous mode of administering the reviving and purifying influence of sea breezes than by the action of these smoothly gliding cars, conducted almost on the sea itself.
[Quote from unknown Brighton Doctor]

Magnus Volk designed, built and operated an electric tourist railway in Brighton without needing any statutory powers, carrying some one million passengers each year by the late 1920s. Quite a contrast to many of the railway stories in this book. And it has a place of honour in *The Guinness Book of Records* as the oldest operational electric railway in the world.

Magnus was the son of a German *émigré* clockmaker who inherited his father's skills and delighted in his workshop. He was an inventor and an engineer. First apprenticed to a scientific instrument maker in 1869, he diversified into making 'parlour telegraphic sets' which he designed himself, including fashionable family amusements which gave mild electric shocks which were all the rage for alleged therapeutic effects. He equipped his house with the first telephone and domestic electric lighting in Brighton, gained a gold medal and was given the job by the local council of installing electric lighting in the Royal Pavillion.

Another German, Werner von Siemens, demonstrated the practicality of electric rail traction at the 1879 Berlin Exhibition and successfully ran a small train in the grounds of London's Crystal palace in 1881. By then Volk had turned his attention turned to developing this and had equipment which he could adapt to deliver it. He convinced the town council to let him build a 2ft gauge passenger line along the sea front in the town from the Palace pier. His railway opened on Saturday 4th August, 1883 when Volk drove the first small car along his new line. On the bank holiday Monday, his electric car ran for eleven hours and carried 1,000 passengers, effectively demonstrating a clean and efficient new form of railway traction to a public then only familiar with horse and steam power.

By today's standards, Volk had established very quickly and simply a workable railway without the constraints, approvals and legislation needed by public railways. He managed to do this simply by securing a lease from the council and by running the railway at high water mark which was outside the jurisdiction of the Board of Trade. He just used his common sense and engineering ingenuity to build his railway and start operating it. He established a gas powered dynamo to feed a 50 volt output direct to a third rail system spiked to well tarred wooden sleepers providing insulation. He laid his railway on shingle ballast for a quarter of a mile from the aquarium eastwards to the Chain Pier, close to the sea wall. Initially, he had just a single car built by a local coach builder capable of carrying ten passengers, finished in varnished mahogany with the initials 'VER' in gold paint on the sides. This could be driven from either end using a rheostat operated by a detachable lever at a maximum speed of around 6mph when fully loaded.

Like many innovations, his railway did not please everybody at first. Many Brighton cabmen saw this novel concept as a rival to their horse drawn cabs, and often railway officials would be worried by the overnight disappearance of some vital part of railway equipment; but each time this happened, they doggedly replaced or repaired it and carried on.

Having proved his concept, Volk negotiated a lease for a new line, this time of 2ft 8 ½ inch gauge, which ran from the Aquarium to the old Chain Pier and, eventually, to Black Rock, with a passing place around halfway allowing for a two-car service. The new saloon cars were a little larger and so could carry more people, but the propulsion arrangements were much the same. They normally ran between 8-10mph, although Volk

The three rail layout of the track with the electrified third rail off centre in the middle. The council have relaid the track in heavier 50lb rail with a mix of wooden and concrete sleepers with a 25lb third rail, mounted on composition insulators. Nowadays the railway is fully fenced off from the public, apart from authorised crossings. [JOHN H. MEREDITH, ROGER CARPENTER COLLECTION]

A fascinating early view with of the promenade in front of the town as a car comes into the terminus at the pierhead. A lady passenger on the front platform is holding onto her wide brimmed hat. On the left tourists sit in a covered horse drawn wagon. On the right, a sign advertises mixed bathing next to wheeled bathing machines used for people to change in and then be wheeled directly into the sea. The use of bathing machines was part of the etiquette for sea-bathing to be observed by both men and women who wished to behave 'respectably'. Especially in Britain, even with the use of the machine to protect modesty, bathing for men and women was usually segregated, so that people of the opposite sex would not see each other in their bathing suits which, although extremely modest by modern standards, were not considered proper clothing in which to be seen in public. [PETER JOHNSON COLLECTION]

The Palace pier terminus looking north east around 1902. Posters advertised Electric Railway cars every six minutes at 4d return. Everything is very simple – just a wooden ticket booth and a sentry box for the ticket collectors, but no shelter at all for passengers. [Michael Whitehouse collection]

The Palace pier terminus station in the early days showing an original polished mahogany car and the wooden platform. The car is full and prospective passengers are waiting. Everyone is well dressed with coats, jackets, hats and with men in white shirts and ties. A small wooden waiting room has now been built for passengers. [John Alsop collection]

Until around 1886, the railway simply ran along the beach on the shingle, with a complete absence of any protection at all from the electric third rail. However, the maximum line voltage of 170 had always been regarded as 'safe' and, anyway, people often touched the live rail for a thrill with no harm arising. The council engineer confirmed that the voltage did not normally exceed 160 when the cars were running and the Board of Trade considered anything below 250v as safe. Just imagine that in the 20th century! [Michael Whitehouse collection]

was certain they could run up to 25-30mph if desired. These cars were likened to a steam yacht on account of their construction in French polished mahogany with an interior comprising décor painted flowers on a panelled ceiling trimmed with gold beading, spring roller blinds with blue and white silk tapes, dark blue silk curtains looped with blue and white silk tassels, blue cushions, gilt framed mirrors, a clock and a barometer.

From 1884 right up until the 1940s, this little railway operated satisfactorily with cars running every five minutes or so, only interrupted by occasional storms or gales. Although it was not quite the first, it was probably the first reliable electric railway. Of course, it was a great novelty and early passengers were fascinated by its electric propulsion. Several people found it hard to understand that its cars could run in two directions when its direct current ran only in one. Volks capitalised on this by producing a penny leaflet explaining its workings, also claiming that a line such as his could be built in three months and make the owner a 25 per cent return on capital employed.

The railway settled down into a reliable and fairly uneventful existence. Volk and the Council entered into an agreement in 1892 exempting the Council from liability, requiring its prior approval to all new works and its agreement if Volk wanted to sell. Inevitably, there was a fatality when a seven-year-old child slipped, fell and burned his neck on the electrified rail in 1915. But Volk was lucky, for although the inquest confirmed death due to electric shock, the child suffered from a physical condition which made him more susceptible to such shocks. The court was told that the maximum line voltage of 170 had always been regarded as 'safe' and that people often touched the live rail for a thrill with no harm arising. The council engineer confirmed that the voltage did not normally exceed 160 when the cars were running and the Board of Trade considered anything below 250v as safe.

By 1926, the railway was literally humming with passengers: 50,000 at bank holiday weekends alone and now a million annually. With some road widening, the line had to be shortened slightly at its western end and a new station at the aquarium was opened in 1930; passenger numbers dropped by 20 per cent, but it increased again when, in 1973, the council opened a new swimming pool at Black Rock.

Up until now, the railway had been worked without any statutory authority, but this changed with the introduction of the Brighton Corporation (Transport) Act in 1938, when the council were empowered to work the railway and it took over completely in 1940, keeping the founder's name.

War intervened of course and, with German invasion threatened, the beach was closed and with it the railway for the duration, but restored again in 1947 with much rebuilding effected to cars, track and stations. Services recommenced in May 1948 and trains ran with two cars rather than singly when required. In 1962, the livery of the cars was changed from varnished mahogany to yellow and dark brown. And traffic stabilised at around half a million passengers a year.

Increased use of the motor car, the advent of overseas package holidays and the closure of Black Rock bathing pool began to reduce traffic and the railway began to return losses. This clearly affected the position as, up until now, the profits had been used to refurbish the line and contribute to the council's coffers and only essential running costs were authorised, resulting in a decline in appearance. By 1971, the Chairman of the Kemp Town Conservation Society was deploring the council's neglect of this historic railway and its dilapidated and squalid conditions. It was kept running on a shoestring basis until the advent of the ill-fated Black Rock Marina project in 1975 and the railway's centenary in 1983.

The council still keeps the railway going – passenger numbers have fallen below 200,000 a year, but it is still there. Fortunately, a supporters' association was formed in 1995 and, in 2014, the National Lottery awarded the railway a grant of £1.6m for a new visitor centre and ticket office at the Aquarium station, a new depot and workshop and the restoration of three cars back to working order.

Of course, there have been many detailed changes, but this little gem of a railway has now run for 140 years with a central and successful purpose: that of moving people from the pier to the marina. That is what seaside railways are all about and we are lucky to have this world beater still alive and running.

Black Rock terminus showing the original simple layout with just two sidings and a wooden hut for a station at the Brighton boundary, looking towards the 'White Cliffs of Old England'. A new more substantial building was built in 1911. [Michael Whitehouse collection]

A car runs along the beach in the 1920s. These views clearly show the elevated line supported on wooden trestles, built firmly against the sea wall and indeed over the sea without any protection on a steel braced timber viaduct. No wonder rides thrilled young passengers, especially when showered by spray from a high tide. Holiday makers are relaxing underneath. [MICHAEL WHITEHOUSE AND JOHN ALSOP COLLECTIONS]

A tram in the new yellow and brown livery runs into the pier terminus station on 9th September, 1961, ready to receive passengers who have arrived by one of the classic road coaches parked alongside. [NEIL PARKHOUSE COLLECTION]

The Oldest Electric Railway in the World: The Volks Electric Railway 115

A tram still in its varnished wood livery runs along the sea front on 9th September 1961. Two lucky passengers sit up front on the open balcony with the driver as the tram is full. [Neil Parkhouse collection]

A re-liveried tram waits at the halfway loop to pass another tram on 9th September 1961. The position of the third electrified rail can clearly be seen. Here the tramway is effectively running along the top of the beach. [Neil Parkhouse collection]

A view to the tram sheds circa 1965. [Neil Parkhouse collection]

Tram at the art deco Marina station on 7th May 1978, now painted in the current livery of yellow and brown. In 1959, there was a proposal to build new cars but it was decided to keep the original ones after careful rebuilding. [Michael Whitehouse collection]

8
THE GOLFERS' TRAMWAY:
THE RYE & CAMBER RAILWAY

You must go to Camber also, Camber being, so to speak, Rye-On-Sea, where the golf links are, and the keddle-nets for mackerel and a long stretch of sands, and the vessels for the fishing fleet where you may lie in the sun and look at the sea, or bathe very peaceably if the tide be not too low and the difficulty of undressing in decent obscurity can be overcome by means of a tent. To get to Camber you take the curious little tram train, which is not the least attraction of the expedition, and the like of which may be met in many parts of Switzerland. Thereby you are saved a dreary two mile walk across the 'Salts'.
[St. James' Gazette, 1906]

Golf has always been a popular hobby for many and, these days, golfers would simply drive to their local club for a game. But not in the 1890s; there were no cars. So it was either walk or ride on horseback to get around. About this time, the game of golf was becoming a popular pastime with the wealthy and this essay will discover the remarkable lengths the residents of Rye went to so that they could enjoy their game, the local seaside sand and social life before the advent of the motor car.

Rye was one of the famous Cinque Ports on the south coast.

Camber on 10th April 1909, after a second major overhaul two years earlier. She was described by the *South Eastern Advertiser* as of '*pretty construction and pattern*'. A diminutive Bagnall 2-4-0T with inside frames, the works No. 1461 was carried on a brass plate fixed to the cabside. Her name originally painted in large serifed gold letters, shaded red, on the side tanks, but is seen here in modified form of ordinary gold letters, again shaded red and complete with full stop after her name. Although ordered to be in a dark blue livery, she arrived in standard Bagnall bright olive green, lined out in black edged red on the outside and white inside, even including on the hinged tramway style motion covering plate. Coupling rods were picked out in red and the interior of the cab painted cream. She was fitted with patent 'link and pin' couplings and safety chains, weighed 6 tons and was capable of hauling 60 tons on the level. Initially she faced chimney first from Rye but very early on was turned to face the other way. The Chairman of the company, Cuthbert Hayes, referred to her as "*an uncommonly good engine*", but two years after delivery she was described as not up to the work with a full train and a busy service, but this may well have been due to a lack of proper maintenance, as she was kept in daily use until *Victoria* arrived as relief. [JOHN ALSOP COLLECTION]

Both Bagnall locomotives together at Rye. As the tramway was worked on the 'one engine in steam' principle, *Camber* is not in steam and *Victoria* had pulled her out of the shed to pose for the photograph, which provides an excellent opportunity for comparison. *Victoria* had essentially been built to the same Bagnall design as *Camber*, but was a little larger and slightly more powerful, most probably taking account of lessons learned from *Camber*'s performance. It may originally have been intended to name her *Rye*, which would be logical and this is shown on the Bagnall 1896 sketch, but presumably in honour of the Queen's Diamond Jubilee, an instruction was sent to Bagnall to name her *Victoria*. Unlike *Camber*, she was delivered in dark blue, lined out in yellow. Her painted name was allowed to fade away and, after the Queen's death in 1901, was never renewed. [H.L. Hopwood, Michael Whitehouse collection]

But, following violent storms in the 13th century, the River Rother was diverted from its course to flow into Rye bay and undermine the eastern side of the town, washing away part of it. Over the next three centuries, altering the outlook of the surrounding marshes so that the sea receded some three miles from the town, creating a considerable area of sand dunes covered with esparto grass.

In the 1890s the town residents investigated the land around the nearby Camber Sands to consider its suitability for developing a golf course. With easy access to the area by means of a bridge over the River Rother opposite Rye harbour, it was agreed to establish a golf course there which was opened on 14th April, 1893. However, even with the new river bridge, it was still a twenty-minute horse and coach drive between Rye and Camber via the circuitous unmade up road. It was quickly clear to the new golf club that to encourage members a more efficient and speedy means of transport was needed. Whilst, nowadays, we would not even consider the concept, the answer at the end of the 19th century was to build a railway; commercially available cars did not then exist.

Influential members of the golf club and local businessmen discussed the idea of building a tramway to serve the Camber golf links and asked the Rye District Council to grant a lease to enable the project which was called The Rye & Camber Tramway Car Company Limited.

The businessmen behind the establishment of the railway company were astute. They included the word 'tramway' in the name clearly seeking to set out their case for derogations from fencing and level crossings which would cost more to maintain. They negotiated a 21-year lease of the requisite land and awarded the construction contract to build a three foot gauge 'tramway' to Holman F. Stephens of light railway fame. As the railway was constructed on private land there was no need for an official Board of Trade inspection. The railway was built, and a steam locomotive named *Camber* and a carriage were ordered from Messrs. W.G. Bagnall of Stafford.

On Saturday, 13th July 1895, steam was raised for the locomotive to be tested, although in truth a few adventurous spirits had a trial trip the day before shortly before midnight after the locomotive had arrived: *'steaming safely out into the darkness and back again' and who could blame them for they were curious and excited.'*

On the Saturday's trial trip, W.H. Austen (Stephens' assistant and another name to conjure with in the field of light railways) acted as driver and, at noon, *Camber* travelled over the whole line and worked 'admirably to everybody's satisfaction', covering the return journey of just over a mile and a half in eight minutes. Naturally, this drew a crowd of local folk who came along for the experience and in the hope of a trip on the new train. The promoters did not hang back in getting started and, at noon on the same day, the Mayoress of Camber declared the tramway open and amidst much cheering from the crowd of well-wishers and a fusillade of fog signals, the little train set off at a rapid pace for Camber with the first section of the company on board. As the train only comprised one carriage with 32 seats, several journeys had to be made to carry all the guests and well-wishers. After the ride, they all adjourned to the Royal William Hotel, past the club house, for an excellent luncheon, of course after grace had been said by the vicar of Rye, the Rev. A.J.W. Crosse, followed by the loyal toast to the Queen and speeches. From incorporation to the day the first train had run was only fourteen weeks; no mean achievement, even if the line was short and simple to build.

The public service began on the following day and, as it was a Sunday, ran only during the afternoon and evening so folk could attend church in the morning. Trains ran hourly with eight minutes allowed for each single journey, but the timetable was not really adhered to that strictly as the objective was to carry all intending passengers.

The tramway settled into its daily routine of taking golfers to the links, day trippers to Camber Sands and fishermen and residents to and from Rye harbour village. The little line was so popular that soon two small wagons had to be pressed into passenger use as well as the single carriage. At the first general meeting, consideration was given to adding a second carriage but the eighty shareholders were initially asked to consider for themselves how many bank holidays' worth of traffic receipts would be necessary to afford that.

The little line did very well from the outset and even declared a dividend of 7 $^1/_2$ per cent for the first year. The board had to admit a 'slight mistake in the figures' in the first annual report which suggested double this dividend would be paid! Talk soon arose about developing Camber Sands further, alongside the other health and seaside resorts then springing up all along the south coast and also extending the tramway to suit. The directors wanted to see a complete year's traffic returns before considering any extension. But they did agree to a second carriage and even considered a second steam locomotive, paid for by issuing further shares and debentures to the town's folk. This locomotive provided back up support for *Camber* which was hauling all the trains every day without any real issue arising, but would of course need time out for occasional maintenance. The new carriage from the Rother Iron Works was delivered in time for Easter 1896 and allowed the tramway to carry 700 passengers on Good Friday and over 2,700 tickets being issued over the Easter weekend; passenger numbers were boosted by season ticket holders. The company hunted around for a second hand locomotive to buy but none were available, so they returned to Bagnalls and ordered a second new one. *Victoria* arrived in June 1897 and entered service straight away, allowing *Camber* to be given some much needed maintenance. The new locomotive was similar to *Camber* but slightly larger and more powerful. Having two locomotives, the tramway was now also able to offer a service on Friday mornings, which had previously seen no service until after lunch, allowing for some time to maintain *Camber*.

The tramway had of course been built for and funded by golfers, as a *pro bono* investment really. The line made a surplus in the summer but lost money during the winter when, of course, people did not go to the beach. This was only really to be expected, but there was still a discussion as to who should pay for this and whether the line should be transferred to the Council so they could ensure the line was always open in the winter for the wider benefit of towns folk by funding it. This conversation was fuelled by the directors (not unreasonably) suggesting that they would like to continue receiving dividends from their investment, rather than the company subsidising the tramway in the winter. This was settled by the golf club agreeing to pay a subsidy to provide a winter service so they could use it to enable year round golf.

The Golfers' Tramway: The Rye & Camber Railway

A view from the early days of the railway showing *Camber* standing at Rye station with both carriages. The locomotive is seen with its original boiler and chimney. The crew have posed for the photographer with conductor Percy Sheppard standing on the platform, whilst 'Jokey' Rhodes, driver & fireman, stands besides the locomotive. It may be winter or certainly a cold and windy day as *Camber* has one cab side sheeted in. [JOHN ALSOP COLLECTION]

Rye station on 10th April 1909. The buildings were all clustered together in a relatively small space, with the locomotive and carriage sheds on the left, whilst *Camber* and its train stand in the platform. The Monk Bretton road bridge can be seen in the left background and the SE&CR's bridge over the River Rother on the right. The original Rye tramway buildings were the shed with the two roof ventilators and the larger of the two station buildings. Note TRAM STATION prominently painted on the corrugated iron roofs, which may have been done as a navigational aid in the early days of commercial aviation. [JOHN ALSOP COLLECTION]

Golf Links Halt. [John Alsop collection]

In 1906 the tramway was extended onto the Camber foreshore terminating at a simple sleeper built platform with no facilities. *Camber*, bedecked with flags, performed the opening ceremony by breaking a red silken cord stretched across the track. Fifty invited guests, comprising directors, shareholders and members of Rye Corporation joined the train and returned to the station at the golf links for afternoon tea in The Retreat close by.

All was going well and continued to do so until the motor car arrived on the scene. A familiar story with nearly all narrow gauge railways and many standard gauge ones too. By 1917 the tramway's winter month receipts had dwindled to an all time low, but the Rye Trade Association came to the rescue with an increased subsidy. Friction began to grow between the tramway company and the golf club. It is easy to see why. The railway was originally largely built for the benefit of the golfers and, indeed, there had been agreement in 1918 that 'it was only just' places should be reserved for golfers on the Sunday 10 o'clock train, particularly as it was effectively paid for by the club. But times were changing. Many visiting golfers were by now using their motor cars to travel to and from the golf links rather than the train. The day tripper had become the company's bread and butter instead.

Bus competition arrived in 1924 from a Rye based family enterprise founded on carting goods to and from London with a horse and wagon. Mr Isaac Wright, who ran this business, handed it over to his son and they bought a 25-seater bus. Unlike the tramway, this was able to offer a door to door service, taking its passengers right into the town of Rye, rather than leaving them half a mile short of their journey and on the wrong side of the river to travel by the tram.

By now the country had been through a terrible war, costs of coal had increased, alternative means of transport were available, and habits were changing. All just like we are experiencing post-pandemic today. The railway company bought a petrol locomotive and lowered its fares. But the golf club discontinued its winter subsidy now cars were all the rage and so winter services ceased. Whilst local people continued to use the tram and patronise the tea room at Camber Sands, further changes were ahead. Several of the tramway's leading figures passed away. The year 1930 was particularly sad in that several of the tramway's closest friends died, including Holman F. Stephens. These were originally the 'middle-aged men', but now in their seventies who, thirty years before, had set up the tramway in the first place and had kept a fatherly eye on proceedings. Characters of the likes of Cuthbert Hayes and John Symonds Vidler shone through the history of the tramway as it unfolded. It seemed now that the tramway, as well, was giving up the will to live as that year its published results declared a loss.

But the summer traffic remained brisk for a while and even Camber Sands station was re-sited. But not for long. Sadly war storm clouds gathered over the English Channel once more and on 3rd September the Second World War was declared. Rather than continue its summer service until the middle of October as usual, the tramway closed the very next day, completely without warning and that was that. Although it was used for a while longer by the Admiralty to move men, equipment and stores in 1943 to service *HMS Haig*, established in Nissan huts adjacent to Rye tram station. The tramway ended in the same way as it began with a jaunt along the line. Rather like the adventurous spirits had taken *Camber* for an explore on the day it first arrived at the very beginning, some sailors 'discovered' the small shed with the petrol locomotive and carriages, got the locomotive running and raced up and down the line 'whooping and cheering like a lot of children…great fun!'

Victoria waits at Camber Sands station on Saturday 10th April 1909 at the head of the tramway's total carriage stock, but with not a soul to be seen. [JOHN ALSOP COLLECTION]

The nearest this commercial postcard can be dated is 8th December 1915 (although it will have been taken before that), as the reverse of the postcard has this date written on it by 'George' sending the card to his mother: *'Received your card also letter quite safe, am having a fine time, this is the Camber tram which runs for about three miles...'* all inscribed in pencil. The image shows a small party of children, maybe a Sunday school outing, posing for the cameraman at Camber Sands station, now complete with a small wooden shelter. On the right of *Camber* the golden sands stretched half a mile to the sea when the tide was out. Just visible under the carriage roofs are brass handrails that, with a footboard along the length of each carriage at platform level, enabled the conductor to walk along the outside of the train to collect the fares whilst it was in motion. Workmen were allowed to travel for 2d, whereas First Class fares were 6d and Second Class 4d. It was left to the discretion of the ticket collector as to whether a passenger could pay First or Second class fares. There was some criticism of this alleging that passengers were charged fares according to their social class. One example of a Captain travelling was given – when in working clothes, he was charged 2d but when in his best suit he was charged the First Class fare of 6d!
[Michael Whitehouse collection]

This is a well known postcard of the tram printed in 1922 in both black & white and tinted colour, which features *Victoria* with all of the passenger rolling stock at Camber Sands. It was a picturesque sight to see the tram running along the embankment, especially at high tide, with the rye water close up to the banks. The train includes the two open wagons fitted with seats which would have been a fun way to travel in the summer season. Although it cannot be seen in the picture, a wooden shack known as Thompson's Tea Rooms was built behind the station in 1922, selling tea, cakes & buns and buckets & spades. Water for it had to be brought out by train as there were no facilities at the station. [Michael Whitehouse collection]

Camber stands at Rye station in 1924 with both carriages and two wagons fitted out to carry passengers. She had now been fitted with a new boiler (in 1921) and her chimney shortened by 4 inches as a result, but her leading pony truck retained the original disc wheels. Her name has vanished from the side tanks and she wears a plain black livery. The hinged plate covering the crosshead and slide bars can be clearly seen, denoting tramway status. The engine is immaculately clean and every available window in the train is open, so it is likely to be a hot summer's day. Percy Sheppard and 'Jokey' Rhodes pose once again for the photograph. The blackboard just inside the waiting room door advised the passengers 'Tickets on the Car'. [MICHAEL WHITEHOUSE COLLECTION]

Golf Course station on 20th June 1950, taken after closure but with the rails still in place. As can be seen, the station building was slowly disintegrating. [ALAN JACKSON, DAVE WALDREN COLLECTION]

A rare sight: the petrol locomotive waiting with both carriages at Rye around 1930. The track and the train look to have been in good order and well presented. An additional double-tracked shed was erected in 1922 and its roof inscribed 'To Camber on Sea', a notation which would really only have been clearly visible from the air. The passengers were all well dressed, so may have been taking a Sunday outing. The Petrol locomotive was built by Kent Construction & Engineering Ltd of Ashford in 1924, Works No. 1364, but was based on the Motor Rail Company's Simplex design. This came about as a result of the Kent Company's purchase of a huge amount of surplus War Department locomotives and parts after the First World War, the most numerous of which were Simplex engines. After refurbishment, they were sold under the 'Planet' trademark but then Kent Construction began new builds based on this same design. The locomotive business was eventually sold to F.C. Hibberd & Co., who carried on with the Planet trademark and maintained the Works numbers sequence. The R&C diesel was scrapped in 1946 but a similar engine, built by Hibberd, Works No. 1568 of 1927, does survive. It was fitted with a water cooled 2-cylinder 20 hp Dorman 2JO engine and the driver sat sideways so he could see the line ahead, whichever way the train was running.
[John Alsop collection]

Open balcony tramcars No's 377, 337, 152 and 340 blink in the sunlight as they peer out of the doorways at Witton Depot on 22nd March 1939. Built by the Borough of Aston Manor, the depot was taken over by the City Corporation from 1st January 1912. [MICHAEL WHITEHOUSE COLLECTION]

9
BIRMINGHAM'S NARROW GAUGE TRAMWAYS

'First impression of Birmingham tram cars – well, they were tall and slim, and looked very smart in their dark blue and cream livery. The ride wasn't bad, better than I had anticipated on the narrow gauge. The Birmingham cars made a distinctive sound. We climbed out of the city at a decent speed and I had the feeling that the motorman of my tram had more power at his command should he choose to use it. At any rate, Birmingham trams were no slouches and we outpaced a number of motor vehicles on our way.'

[Ralph Smith]

In late Victorian times, the West Midlands consisted of several towns and villages ranging over three counties: Warwickshire, Staffordshire and Worcestershire. Rapid industrialisation and the growth of Birmingham as a city largely brought all these areas together and several smaller local authorities were merged into Birmingham, which was granted city status by Queen Victoria in 1889. The area had a huge interconnected 3ft 6 inch gauge tramway system and, during its life, unusually operated horse, steam, cable accumulator and electric tramcars between 1881 and 1953.

On 7th August 1860, an American by the name of George Francis Train (yes, really) promoted a tramway scheme in Birmingham but failed to generate any enthusiasm for his project. However, by the following year, the city gained statutory powers to begin construction and the Tramways Act, 1870 more or less simultaneously laid down the rules and regulations for tramways and encouraged local authorities to construct the permanent way, but left it open for private companies to operate. The effect of this legislation had similarities to today's passenger train franchise system on the national railway network. The Act empowered local authorities to acquire tramways in their region after twenty-five years, by negotiation. This inhibited private companies from investing in their infrastructure and equipment as they could not be sure of a long term future for their business. Of course, this gave the city the upper hand it later sought and achieved.

The region's tramway revolution began in the 1880s, although the first horse tram route had already begun in 1872 as standard gauge from Hockley, just outside the city centre, to West Bromwich and Dudley Port and then from Colmore Row, right in the central business district, along the Bristol Road artery to Bournbrook.

As we all know, the industrial revolution was based on steam power and Birmingham was right at the centre of developing this technology; Boulton & Watt playing a crucial part. By the 1870s, steam power was reliable and well understood

The *Ian Allan 'abc'* of Birmingham City Transport, retailing at 2s 6d. This had an introduction written by W.A. Camwell, the well known tram enthusiast who was also Secretary to the Midland Area of the Stephenson Locomotive Society and organised a large number of special trains in the region. This little booklet gave a concise history of the city's trams, a description of each type of tram, a fleet list (for red lining) and a list of depots and routes, together with a comprehensive route map. Motor buses were dealt with in a companion volume.
[MICHAEL WHITEHOUSE COLLECTION]

A steam tram towing Falcon trailer No. 45 travels out of the city centre along Moat Row, a short street boasting two pubs, in around 1882; the tram was only going as far as Sparkbrook. The trailer has two doors at the top of the staircase so passengers can get to both sides of the knifeboard seating and the upper deck is fitted with 'decency screens' on its sides but not on the ends. The Georgian buildings behind were nearing the end of their useful lives. The coffee house also sold tea and hot pies. [MICHAEL WHITEHOUSE COLLECTION]

A Kitson steam tram and Falcon trailer stand in the road at Perry Bar around 1906, shortly before the lease for operating steam trams came up for renewal. The small boy on the pavement is wearing a sailor suit made popular in 1846 by Queen Victoria's decision to dress the four-year-old Prince Albert similarly. [MICHAEL WHITEHOUSE COLLECTION]

Birmingham's Narrow Gauge Tramways

Corporation Street, Birmingham

A steam tram with double decked trailer trundles down Corporation Street in Birmingham City centre. Apart from the tram, only a horse and cart and a bicycle can be seen on this main city centre road, and note that everything was clean and tidy and everyone smartly dressed. This Valentine's postcard shows the city at the height of its business development towards the end of the Victorian era, grand buildings, the Wesylan and General Assurance Company on the left and the law courts in the background. At this time, the city was in the good hands of largely non-conformist businessmen who believed both in making profits for their firms and ensuring their workers were well treated, thereby creating a city to be proud of. Not for nothing did Birmingham's city crest include workers of both sexes with the tools of their trade and the motto 'Forward'. How times have changed. [MICHAEL WHITEHOUSE COLLECTION]

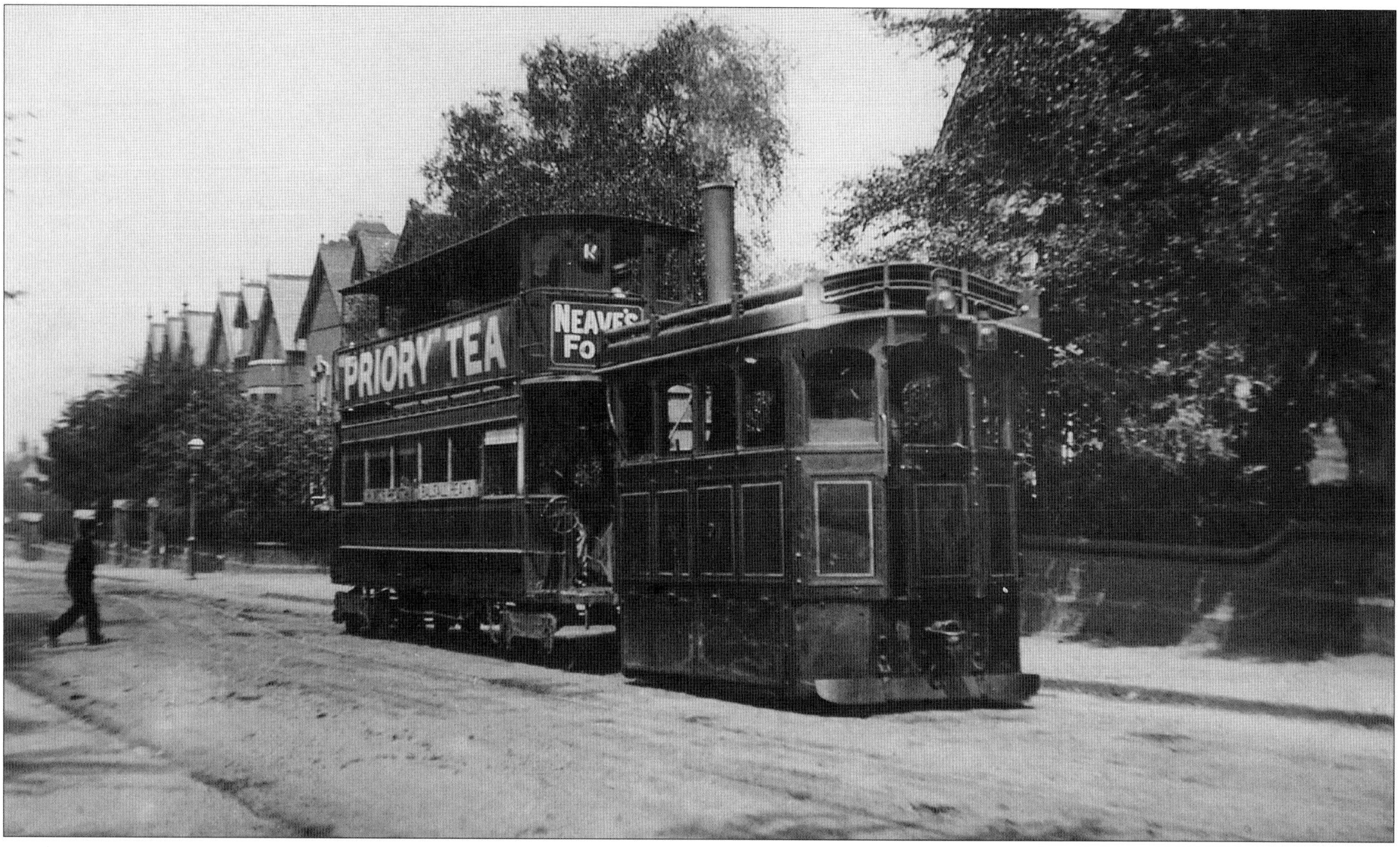

Kitson steam tram No. 73, built in 1894, runs firebox first whilst towing one of the first series Falcon canopy-topped, double-deck bogie saloons built in 1884 with knifeboard seating. The trailer displays the letter K, signifying it is running on the Kings Heath via Balsall Heath route, confirmed by the boards on the side of the car. The sun glints off the top of the steam tram which is standing at the Augustus Road loop in Park Road. [MICHAEL WHITEHOUSE COLLECTION]

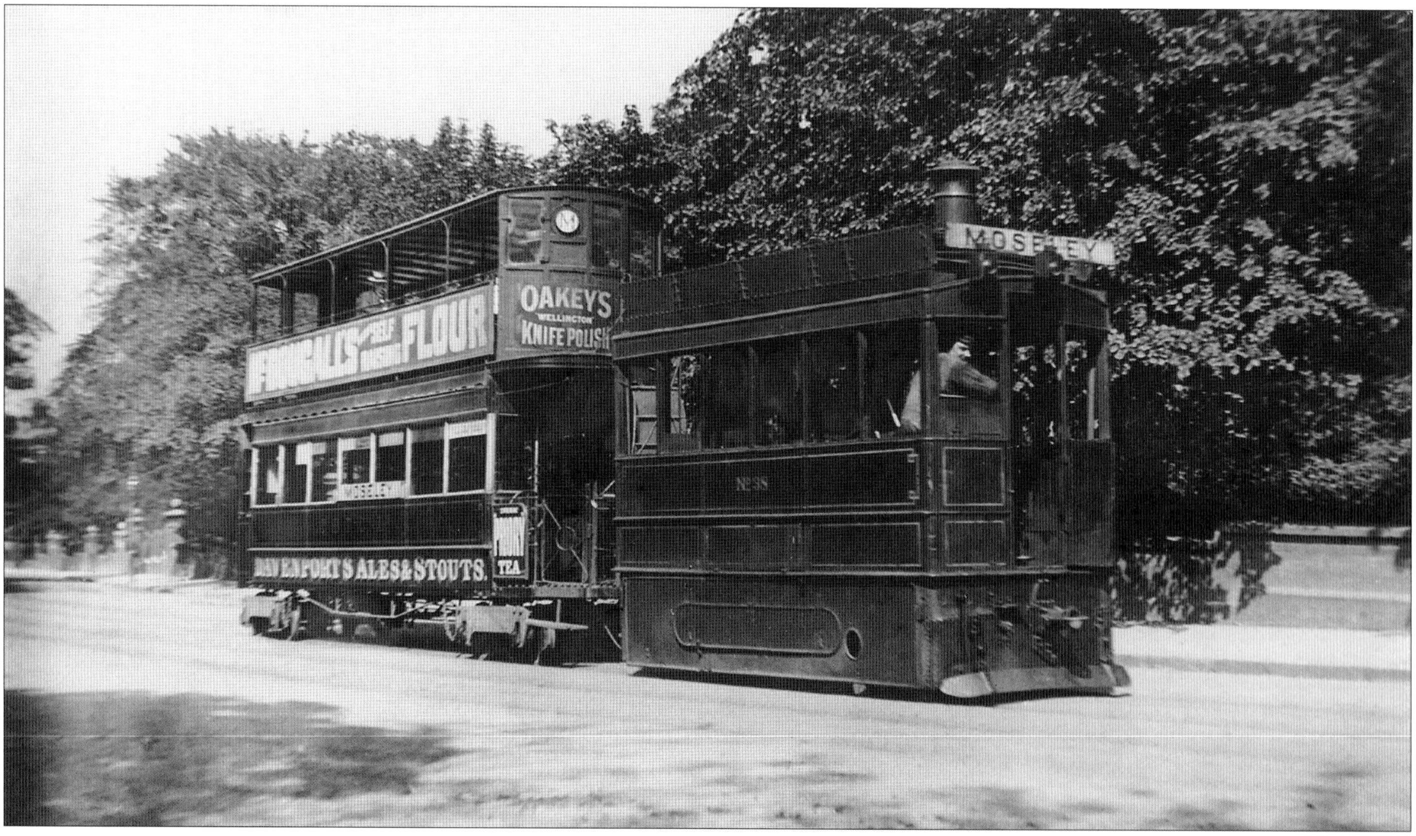

Kitson steam tram No. 38 runs along the Moseley Road bound for the village in the early 1900s, towing a double-decked trailer car fitted with 'modesty' boards covered with advertising to shield ladies who ventured onto the upper deck. Moseley was a 'well-to-do' suburb of the city. [MICHAEL WHITEHOUSE COLLECTION]

A steam tram and trailer stand at the crossroads in the centre of Moseley village in 1902, also with the tram engine running firebox first, whilst on its way from town to Kings Heath. Two ladies climbed the external stairs of the trailer whilst other passengers waited to board. This trailer, Falcon No. 18, was by now eighteen years old and to put this in a modern context, few buses last this long. A smartly dressed lady with a parasol umbrella crosses the road in front of the tram. In the background is St. Mary's Row with the 15th century tower of St. Mary's parish church. [Michael Whitehouse collection]

by both civil and mechanical engineers, although, before steam trams could venture out onto the streets amongst the population, designers had to convince the authorities that boiler explosions, bolting horses, frightened pedestrians, excessive speeds, unpleasant smoke and fumes could be mitigated or avoided altogether. It is to the credit of the local authorities that a uniform track gauge of 3ft 6 ins was adopted for what was to be rapid expansion of an interurban steam tramway, by leasing their tracks to private companies with the Board of Trade usually granting steam operating licences for seven years at a time.

Kitson and Falcon provided the steam trams for many years. But, by the late 1890s, following the incorporation of the British Electric Traction Company (BET), which was to become a major force in public transport both in Britain and the Empire, schemes were already being assembled to create an extensive electric tramway network. This would cross county and parish boundaries and connect with the City of Birmingham's tracks. BET championed overhead wires which were installed and the next evolution began. In 1902, BET acquired the City of Birmingham Tramways Co., but Walsall and Wolverhampton ran their own systems, all defeating a proposition to construct an underground network, as in London. Leases were granted to operate these routes and some negotiations for these produced less than perfect results. BET's vision of an interconnecting network sometimes overlooked the need for a constructive dialogue with Birmingham Corporation.

By 1903, the political pendulum had swung the other way, towards municipally owned and operated tramway systems, resulting in the Birmingham Corporation Act, 1903 which allowed the city to become its own tramway operator. The city then never looked back. It appointed Alfred Baker to get on with the job and he certainly did. He was a man who preferred to listen to reasoned argument and then to reach a consensus. He instituted a business like approach to dealings with BET and also set to work organising reconstruction of existing steam lines and the building of new electric routes.

'Personally, I have always held it is quite a proper and simple thing to make mutual arrangements for one authority to run into the area of another. In Birmingham we have at the present moment running powers with several outside authorities...and I may tell...that there is not a scrap of paper between us, nothing in the nature of an agreement, and yet we run into each other's areas without the slightest difficulty or trouble.' [Alfred Baker]

For the new electric tramway system, double track was the norm and trackwork was to the highest standards to allow an intensive service (although the Black Country persisted with single track and loops).

The preference was for 4-wheeled, single-truck, electric cars with two motors as they were better suited to the sharp curves and gradients of the city routes. On 14th April, 1906, Roseberry Street Depot opened with the first cars: a batch of 50 built by the United Electric Car Co. of Preston. Each car seated 22 people in the lower saloon and 26 on the top deck. A further 130 Brill cars were ordered between 1905-8, followed by a large number of radial tram cars, No's 71-220, with the Birmingham

A steam tram runs through Smithfield market around 1890.
[Photographer unknown]

A scene on the Alcester Road with a steam tram amongst several horse drawncarts and a coach. A group of children pose for the photographer, who would have required them to stand still, although the lad slightly out of focus on the left seems to have got bored and started to move away. The photographer would have set up a tripod to take this picture with a plate glass camera. This is a commercial postcard published in the famous Valentine's Series. [MICHAEL WHITEHOUSE COLLECTION]

Birmingham's Narrow Gauge Tramways

Light Railway and Canal, Kinver.

On Good Friday, 5th April 1901, the British Electric Tramway Company opened a new line from the village of Kinver to Coalbournbrook, where a connection was made with the Dudley, Stourbridge & District trams. The Kinver Light Railway ran on its own private right of way beside the Staffordshire & Worcester Canal on one of the country's most picturesque tram routes. Here we see DS&DTC car No. 43 running amongst the trees with not a house in sight. Kinver Edge was a popular beauty spot and thus could now be reached of tens of thousands of town dwellers, who were able to journey to this magical place by tramcar. [JOHN ALSOP COLLECTION]

'Toastrack' tram No. 51 stands at Kinver. The tram crew pose for the photographer: the driver has his hand on the control lever whilst the conductor stands adjacent with his pouch slung around his shoulder. [JOHN ALSOP COLLECTION]

Electric tram No. 165 makes its way along the new Bristol Road. This route boasted long straight sections and, in the early years, the road was almost devoid of traffic. The overhead wires were put up with a view to minimising their effect on the townscape. The new electric tramway had pride of place with no other traffic in sight; a far cry from today's congestion. [MICHAEL WHITEHOUSE COLLECTION]

Electric tram No. 206 makes its way down Stirchley High Street circa 1905. Note that maintenance work was underway on one of the poles carrying the overhead wires, whilst on the opposite side of the road a discussion was underway with the top-hatted driver of a pony and trap. [Michael Whitehouse collection]

A 4-wheeled tram car pauses at Aston Cross whilst a horse-drawn van moves towards the junction. A second open-topped tram is partially concealed by the van. The design of the postbox in front of the clock hardly changed in a hundred years. [MICHAEL WHITEHOUSE COLLECTION]

Birmingham's saddest tramway event for many a year came on 1st October 1907 when Car No. 22 ran out of control down the 1 in 17 gradient in Warstone Road and overturned on the curve into Hingeston Street. Two passengers were killed and seventeen others injured. The cause was traced to the failure of the magnetic brake due to a faulty rheostat. [MICHAEL WHITEHOUSE COLLECTION]

Corporation firmly nailing their colours to the mast in developing the system. Efficient management of the enlarged fleet resulted in the development of Kyotts Lake Works as the central facility, originally built for steam trams.

Meanwhile discussions had been going on to create a Greater Birmingham under one unitary authority, incorporating the urban districts of Quinton & Harborne, East Birmingham, Yardley, South Birmingham, Sutton Coldfield, Rubery and Oldbury. This had a very important consequence for the development of the tramway system, as a priority was to create suburbs to rehouse citizens away from unsanitary slum conditions which had built up around the factory developments within the city centre.

With the passing of the Greater Birmingham Act, 1911, the city now aspired to become the second city in the Empire. Strategic city planning began. George Cadbury, a very influential local businessman, reported on the planning of suitable roads – both ring and radial – land use allocation and the provision of open spaces. Allowance was made for tramways to run down the sides or roadways and within central reservations, so providing many advantages over other systems. Alfred Baker sought and gained authority to acquire a further 60 single-truck trams. And from 1912 Birmingham Corporation Tramways was finally master in its own house, owning and operating system-wide.

Before the First World War, the British tram car was in ascendancy. The notion that the motor bus could ever challenge this efficient mode of transport was dismissed as fantasy. Electric traction was a proven and reliable technology; fares were cheap and services frequent. Huge crowds attending football matches were dealt with swiftly and efficiently by lines of tramcars at Villa Park, St. Andrews and the Hawthorns. Many 'Brummies' took the Bristol Road tram out to the Lickey Hills near Rednal, for weekend walks in the large natural park and summer resort. The circular tramway turning circle there survived for many years after end of the tramway.

As we have seen in other essays, the First World War changed everything, just as the recent pandemic is doing now. Negative consequences for both were price inflation and shortages, both of materials and foodstuffs. Technology changes also occur as a result of war and, after the 1914-18 period, the motor car and lorry had become a much more serious commercial proposition. But the city persisted with tramways, quite rightly as we now see with their reintroduction coming apace in the modern world after the incursion by the motor bus. George Cadbury explains why, quite simply:

'The trams, having an unobstructed route, can travel more quickly from point to point, and being generally alongside a footpath the passengers are saved the necessity of crossing the road, with all its attendant risks and disadvantages. The reason

Electric 8-wheel (bogie) tram No. 803, which was powered by two 60 hp motors, runs along Route 36 between Navigation Street and the suburb of Cotteridge. On the right is an advert for the well-known Birmingham-based Mitchells & Butlers' brewery, which had its own private siding and connected to the Harborne Railway. [MICHAEL WHITEHOUSE COLLECTION]

that separate tramway tracks have not been provided before is that towns have not looked far enough ahead, and have delayed taking trams out until the road is so built in that a separate track cannot be provided.'

By 1912, Baker turned his attention to ordering bogie trams and the first entered service in the next year. The system gained a reputation with these tall stately double-decked trams for being clean and smart in appearance, as well as being mechanically sound. The Kyotts Lake Road Works was renowned for its efficiency; it kept its trams looking smart and in top condition which, in turn, resulted in a minimum number of breakdowns on the street. Under Baker's stewardship, Birmingham Corporation Tramways expanded to provide the city and suburbs with a highly efficient transport system. Whilst electric trams formed the backbone, motor buses and electric trolleybuses were also being developed. By 1918, receipts topped a million pounds for the first time with passenger figures at 402, 908.

Significant investment in the tramway system continued. A new depot was opened at Selly Oak in July, 1927 and heralded as one of the best of its kind in the country. Situated in Harborne Lane it cost £27,000 and had capacity for 80 trams and buses with the trams on ten roads, although the buses were soon transferred to another depot at Acocks Green.

Whilst, the city's trams were built to last and could give several lifetimes of public service, this was eventually to be their undoing. Trams which were modern in the early 1900, became distinctly old-fashioned when compared with buses in the 'streamline era' of the 1930s, although the narrow width of the tram was a constraint more apparent than real; the ride was smoother than many systems elsewhere due to sound construction and good maintenance. But clearly steps had to be taken to make travelling by tram a more attractive proposition. So protection was provided for top deck passengers, who previously had to sit in the open air. This resulted in a fug caused by cigarette smokers which had to be dissipated by opening the windows.

Outside the city, the neighbouring Black Country tramways had entered into a terminal spiral of decline. In the 1930s, a bus network, marketed under the name Midland Red, was being expanded. In Parliament, serious moves were afoot to ensure that the tramcar had no future in British urban transport:

'Tramways, if not an obsolete form of transport, are at all events in a state of obsolescence, and cause much unnecessary congestion and considerable danger to the public. Therefore, we recommend that no additional tramways should be constructed, and that, though no definitive time limit can be laid down, they should gradually disappear and give place to other forms of transport.' [Royal Commission on Transport, 1931.]

This was music to the ears of the motor and oil industries. Furthermore, the tram tracks all laid within a relatively short period of time and having seen intensive use, were

No. 726, another 8-wheel bogie tram, but this time powered by two 40 hp motors, meets its new omnibus competitor. Registrarion No. JOJ 34 was one of the first 'new look' front streamliners with a Metro Cammell H54R body and Daimler CD6 engine, built in 1950. [MICHAEL WHITEHOUSE COLLECTION]

Nearly the end with, despite appearances to the contrary, single line working now in place. Tram No. 829, built in 1928 as a totally enclosed car by Short Bros, mounted on Maley & Taunton 'Burnley' type bogies and fitted with both air and track brakes, passes a row of stored trams in Pebble Mill Road on 7th June 1952. [J.H. MEREDITH, MICHAEL WHITEHOUSE COLLECTION]

W.A. Camwell, took this picture from the top deck of tramcar No. 343 approaching Six Ways, Aston on 12th July 1949. In front of the imposing National Provincial Bank building. It is following No. 694 which has already crossed the junction on its way to Tyburn Road. Meanwhile, No. 604 on service 5 from Gravelly Hill approaches, whilst No. 452 waits for the junction to clear before crossing on its way to Perry Bar. This tram, along with its sister No. 451, was then the oldest in service, originally built as an open top car in 1903. They were nicknamed 'Titanics' as they were longer than other cars in use.
[W.A. CAMWELL, MICHAEL WHITEHOUSE COLLECTION]

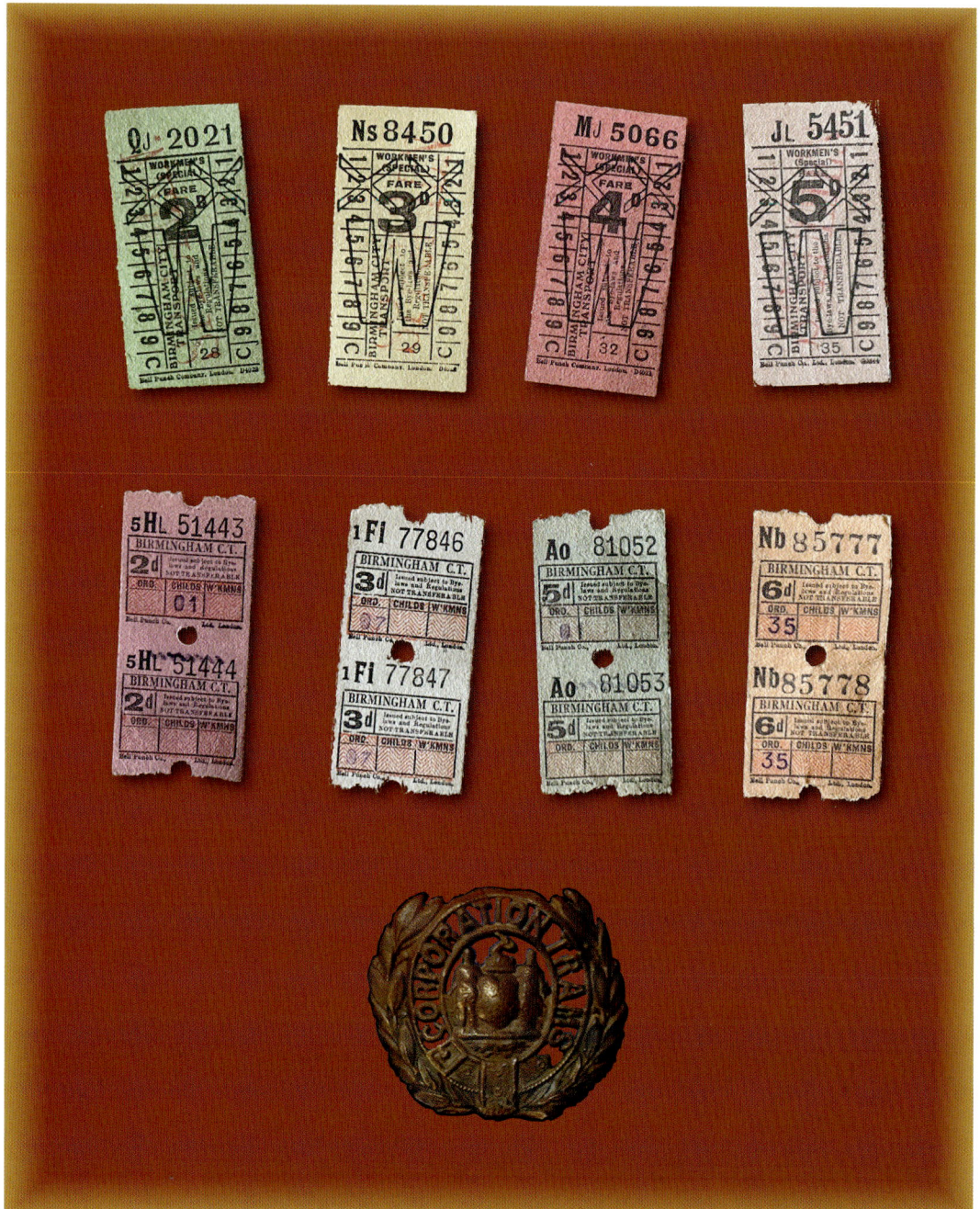

A collection of Birmingham tram tickets. The four at the top of the picture are Workmen's Specials and the four below are the standard issue tickets. These could be clipped for issue to adults, children or workmen and each of the four in the picture had been hole punched for use. The tickets were printed by the Bell Punch Co. Ltd, London.
[MICHAEL WHITEHOUSE COLLECTION]

now beginning to require wholesale replacement. The tide was turning against the tramcar. The arrival of the reliable AEC Regent buses from 1929 doomed the Birmingham tram, although there was a temporary reprieve for the duration of the Second World War.

The Transport Committee's Annual Report for 1946 showed 462 trams, 74 trolleybuses and 1,202 buses in the fleet. But it was now time to say farewell the Birmingham City tram (at least for now). Whilst tramway enthusiasts pressed for two sets of routes to form a rapid transit system with a fleet of modern PCC single deck cars, the concept went down like a lead balloon with BCT and the Council. Government grants were available to buy new diesel buses. 'Last tram week' was very low key, car 395 was transferred to the new Museum of Science and Industry and enthusiasts gathered on Saturday, 28th June 1953 for the farewell tour with cars 616 and 623. Trams still ran in commercial service for a little while longer. Car 616 was chosen to bring down the final curtain, leaving Steelhouse Lane depot at 10.48am on Saturday 4th July.

The diesel bus had been given a leading role in post war planning. In Birmingham, the motor car industry had long taken over from steam powered industry and in the 1960s, the city engineer and surveyor, Herbert Manzoni, re-engineered the inner city roadway system for the car with even pedestrians relegated to subways and dark passages. It is only recently, these urban design mistakes have been realised and the 'concrete collar' of the inner ring roads broken and tramways brought back into the city.

10
THE RAILWAY FROM NOWHERE TO NOWHERE:
THE LEEK & MANIFOLD RAILWAY

'The fundamental idea of light railway construction and working is the elimination of every kind of expenditure which is non-essential to its efficiency as a means of transport, and the reduction of all permanent way, works, plant and appliances to their simplest and most inexpensive forms.'
E.R. Calthrop

Walking through the beautiful Manifold Valley today, along the route once used by the delightful 2ft 6 inch gauge narrow gauge railway running past the intriguing Thor's Cave, it is somewhat difficult to conceive how such a railway would not be sought after by tourists if still running today. Unfortunately, it is not still running. The sad fact of life is that the Leek & Manifold Railway never really made any money and ended up running from nowhere to nowhere. But it did provide public transport for people who previously had none and also a social need, even though it did not also provide a financial return. The promoters were local businessmen, keen to open up and develop the Manifold Valley. They achieved their objective to a point, but at a terrible financial sacrifice. No dividend was ever paid to the shareholders and, in later years, the directors were reduced to considering an appeal to the public for donations towards paying off the bank overdraft.

The Leek & Manifold Valley Light Railway was opened for passenger traffic by Lord Dartmouth on Monday, 27th June 1904. The railway was nine miles long and provided access to one of the loveliest and least known valleys in Staffordshire, whilst forming a feeder line for the standard gauge North Staffordshire Railway.

The construction of the Manifold line was largely sponsored by local people caught up in the railway mania who wanted a railway of their own. It is reported that a local councillor even invited the directors of the North Staffordshire Railway to a good luncheon at his home and then took them for a drive along the road to Waterhouses 'coincidentally' on market day so passing an endless stream of traffic! The NSR did agree to operate the railway for the private company, but there was friction from the start between the directors' starry eyed objectives and the NSR's desire to operate the line economically. In all probability the original working arrangement was unrealistic from the outset: the NSR were obliged to hand over 45 per cent of gross receipts to the owning company without any deduction for working expenses. These receipts were not all they might have been, as the only passenger access from Leek was by a rather unreliable steam bus. A proposal by the NSR to raise fares was rejected and further friction arose as the NSR considered it only feasible to operate on three days a week, whereas the railway company wanted two trains every day of the week in winter and three in summer, which was eventually agreed to.

The directors then wanted to extend the line to Buxton. Whilst this might perhaps have made a difference to the traffic carried, the NSR flatly refused to the proposal beyond Longnor and, with the railway's financial position becoming serious even by 1907, this proposal was dropped.

The railway's main passenger traffic did not originate from

The elaborate company seal of the Leek & Manifold Valley Light Railway Company, designed by Edward Challinor and Sir Thomas Wardle and supplied by the well-known company stationers, Jordan & Co., at a cost of £4 7s 6d, including a lockable japanned wooden case. The seal incorporated the Staffordshire knot and an impression of a meandering river, together with Thor's Cave.

The Kitson-built 2-6-4T No. 2 named *J.B. Earle*. Earle, who it was named after, worked for Calthrop, first as an assistant and then as a partner, developing railways overseas, particularly in Mexico and India, having previously trained as a civil engineer with Sir Douglas Fox & Partners. The photograph shows the engine when new, together with a transporter wagon, both on test shortly after arrival in June 1904. *J.B. Earle* was seen in original chocolate brown fully lined out livery, with the two tall hooters as originally fitted in front of the cab, together with the Ramsbottom safety valves on top of the dome; these were replaced in about 1912 as the sound did not carry well within the narrow valleys. The train has been posed in Ladyside Wood, between Grindon and Thor's Cave. The picture also shows Calthrop's method of railway construction in narrower sections, with the formation partly cut into the hillside and partly above a retaining wall built into the river. [MICHAEL WHITEHOUSE COLLECTION]

the locality. Even from the outset, a large proportion of the traffic was foreseen as being tourist day trippers. In practice the line could (and did) carry more traffic in one Stoke Wakes Week than in the whole of the rest of the year put together, but this was not conducive to good accounting and profit making. Whilst dairy traffic propped up revenues for a while, only eleven years after the railway was absorbed by the London Midland & Scottish Railway, it succumbed.

The authorisation and construction of the railway was made possible by The Light Railway Act passed in August, 1896 for the purpose of 'facilitating the construction of light railways' which would be 'found beneficial to the rural districts'. The Act enabled Government and Local Authorities to provide financial assistance to railway promoters and for lines to be built under the auspices of secondary legislation, pursuant to Light Railway Orders, so saving the costs of a special Act of Parliament, together with some construction concessions to reduce the capital outlay in return for lower operating speeds to manage the safety risk.

Almost certainly, special interest in the Leek & Manifold Railway comes from its engineer's approach. E.R. Calthrop came to the railway by chance. He was a man with strong opinions and sound railway experience. He was the consulting engineer for the Indian Barsi Light Railway built to the 2ft 6in. gauge in 1897. He had then been asked by the Light Railway Commissioners to advise on the Leek & Manifold proposal as they were unimpressed by the original scheme put to them by the promoters. Whilst Calthrop was making his report, the railway's engineer died and, as Calthrop advised that considerable savings could be made in the execution of the railway works, he was asked to take up the engineer's mantle and did so to good effect. He had little difficulty in imposing his views on the inexperienced and receptive directors and to good effect.

Calthrop's view was that, if light railways were to be developed in Britain, the narrow gauge was essential to obtain the maximum cost advantage. Actually, he went further than that, by advocating in a paper delivered to the Institute of Engineers in 1897 that a central organisation ought to be

E.R. Calthrop stands at Hulme End in original chocolate brown livery with a passenger train. The line's resident engineer, John B. Earle, poses in the middle of the group of three people by the front of the locomotive. [JOHN ALSOP COLLECTION]

Early postcard showing the entirety of Hulme End station, all very neat and well kept. The locomotive and carriage sheds are on the right and a train is waiting to depart. [John Alsop collection]

This North Staffordshire Railway steam bus connected with the Leek & Manifold train at Waterhouses. Although the roadway was not yet metalled, this mode of transport, along with its successor motorbuses and cars, was to prove more convenient than the narrow gauge railway. At most stations, excepting Hulme End and Sparrowlee, there was a long walk downhill to the train, thus, coming home, a long climb back up with the week's shopping. It was therefore no wonder that the farm and carrier's carts still flourished, especially as the overall journey time by each form of transport was about the same. The petrol-driven road vehicle completely killed the local Manifold passenger service. [John Alsop collection]

The Railway from Nowhere to Nowhere: The Leek & Manifold Railway

A view of Waterhouses from Brown End Quarry circa 1906, showing both the North Staffordshire and Leek & Manifold railways and their juxtaposition. [JOHN ALSOP COLLECTION]

A train for Hulme End departs from Grindon soon after the railway opened in June 1904. At the front are the first two carriages to be delivered, one of each type (a Composite First/Third Brake and an all Third), both in the original primrose yellow livery, along with two of the transporter wagons here seen carrying standard gauge wagons. The open coal wagon is a wrought iron one built by Robert Heath & Sons, owners of several Staffordshire collieries, and the Biddulph Valley Ironworks. Four carriages were supplied of two types: two Composites providing eight First Class and twenty-two Third Class seats with a guard's compartment, and two Third Class only carriages, with accommodation for forty-four passengers. All the carriages were provided with end balconies, automatic vacuum brakes and electric lighting. The primrose yellow of L&M days gave way to maroon under LM&SR days. On fine days, the end balconies were popular with the public who were allowed to ride on them. Sometimes, passengers riding immediately behind the locomotive would torment the footplate crew by throwing orange peel or apple cores but there was a sure fire remedy for this. At Butterton, a lump of oily cotton waste would be thrown into the firebox, the door shut just as the regulator was opened and the train plunged into the darkness of Swainsley Tunnel. Emerging into the sunlight, there would not be a sign of anyone on the balcony and all the carriage doors and windows would be firmly shut! [MICHAEL WHITEHOUSE COLLECTION]

created to manage all the light railways in any one country so as to gain economies of scale. He stressed the need for standard components and rolling stock. To some extent he was advocating going further than the Board of Trade's light railway powers.

He reduced the construction estimate for the railway by £11,000 by means of his patent system of adopting uniformity of axle load for all equipment, thus reducing the weight and so the cost of the track, adopting a maximum uniform load of five tons per axle to run on rails with a minimum weight of only 30lbs per yard at an ordinary speed of 15mph.

The Leek & Manifold locomotives and carriages were almost carbon copies of the Barsi Light Railway and built to the very limits of the loading gauge. Maybe this was not surprising as that line too followed Calthrop's patent system, so savings would also have been made by adopting the same designs from that railway, which were both functional and aesthetically beautiful, as well probably as being to a higher standard than usual for British light railways.

Two steam locomotives were built by Kitson of Leeds, handsome 2-6-4Ts, the first of this wheel arrangement in Britain, and originally painted in an attractive chocolate brown livery and ornately lined out with double white lining. These Manifold locomotives turned out to be modelled on the Kitson 'tropical' design for the Barsi Light Railway, even down to the double roofed cab (to mitigate hot weather) and the front headlamp which was never needed or used in the Manifold valley. It appeared that Kitson's were instructed to build a 2-6-4T 'like a Barsi engine' and did so.

The carriages also followed the Indian pattern and were, unusually and startlingly, painted primrose yellow. These proved to be a good colour match with the locomotives. They were built by the Electric Railway and Tramway Carriage Works of Preston, the forerunners of English Electric. They

J.B. Earle and one of the Composite Brake carriages pose for an official photograph on bridge No. 15 over the River Hamps at Redhurst. Two ladies pose inside the locomotive's cab. Everything is still new and the dry stone walling is in pristine condition. [MICHAEL WHITEHOUSE COLLECTION]

were unusually large bogie open saloons, lit by electricity and with end balconies. At holiday times the original four carriages were insufficient for the day tripper traffic and so were augmented by fitting seats to the open goods and also to the transporter wagons. The Manifold line became popular for Saturday excursions from the smoke-laden Potteries and timetables were augmented from three returns to six or seven trips on such days, requiring both locomotives to be used in the peak holiday months of July and August.

Calthrop continued his innovations in relation to the railway's freight stock, tackling head on the issue of transshipment from the standard gauge North Stafford Railway at Waterhouses. Having designed the line to accommodate carriages nearly as wide as contemporary main line passenger vehicles, he designed an ingenious transporter wagon which saved any unloading and reloading by the simple device of carrying the standard gauge wagon piggy back on a narrow gauge wagon. These transporter wagons were the only ones of their type in Britain and proved most satisfactory and rode well at speed.

Calthrop's Manifold experiment is perhaps of more interest for what did not happen elsewhere, but might have been. His patent design could have been applied as a template for a wider application of the 2ft 6in. gauge in Britain for light railways and rural lines, rather than construction on the standard gauge. Indeed, the Duke of Sutherland, on hearing the plaudits of the narrow gauge over dinner at the Oakley Arms Hotel on the occasion of Fairlie's double engine trials on the Festiniog Railway, wished he had spent less money by building narrow gauge railways in his Scottish highlands. One might imagine a whole network of narrow gauge minor lines constructed to Calthrop design all over Britain, but this was not to be. In reality, the Light Railway Act only enabled unconnected lines to be built in less populated areas of the country as standard gauge had already taken a major hold. But the concept did take off in other countries.

So, the Calthrop experiment, whilst interesting and effective from a textbook view point, unfortunately turned out to be a white elephant, specifically so on the railway it was developed for which ran from nowhere to nowhere. Whilst India, where Calthrop cut his teeth on narrow gauge railway design, built an extensive metre gauge railway network, even that is now nearly all converted to broad gauge in so far as it survives at all.

Most certainly, the Leek & Manifold is fondly remembered for the magnificent scenery it ran through, Thor's Cave, the beautiful large steam engines, the ornate and unusually liveried carriages and the intriguing transporter wagons. But the railway did not generate the traffic to pay its way and nor could it have done. There was simply not enough traffic, especially once the dairy at Ecton closed down. The LMS took little time in shutting its only narrow gauge inheritance down. Much of the route of the railway lives on as a footpath.

Beeston Tor station in 1906 with a train utilising railway's entire rolling stock, apart from the covered van, to accommodate all the excursionists bound for Hulme End. Just above the locomotive can be seen the refreshment room managed by Billy Wood from Beeston Tor Farm, in the valley.
[Michael Whitehouse collection]

E.R. Calthrop pauses at Thor's Cave station with a train for Waterhouses on Thursday 25th April 1907. The footplate crew are nowhere to be seen but a young lad in starched white collar has climbed aboard the locomotive for the photograph. The new corrugated steel refreshment room is on the right of the picture selling bottles of soda water, lemonade and lime juice. [MICHAEL WHITEHOUSE COLLECTION]

A Calthrop-designed transporter wagon, which enabled standard gauge wagons to be carried over the 2ft 6 inch gauge railway with simplest of transshipment arrangements. [H.W. ROBINSON, PETER JOHNSON COLLECTION]

Hulme End station probably soon after the opening of the railway, depicted in a colourised photograph issued as a North Staffordshire Railway 'official' postcard. Standing by the ornate station sign, *E.R. Calthrop* is in the original chocolate brown livery, fully lined out, which extended to the headlamp, fly cranks and axle centres. Joseph Edwards, the first driver on the line, stands on the footplate and, on the ground beside him is Matthew Haycock, the stationmaster at Hulme End. Edwards was responsible for the day-to-day running of the railway. [Michael Whitehouse collection]

The North Staffordordshire realised the potential of the Manifold Valley for tourism and devoted eight of its official postcards to the railway. This card features a three-coach train alongside the river near Thor's cave. The image was later reissued as a black & white framed picture placed in railway carriage compartments entitled 'River, Train and Cliff'. [Michael Whitehouse collection]

Probably the same train, this time posed at the halt for Thor's Cave which can be seen high on the hillside above the Manifold Valley. The most photographed location in the valley and featured on dozens of Edwardian postcards, the great domed cave is a remnant of an Ice Age subterranean cave system of vast proportions with evidence that it was once a Neolithic burial chamber.
[Michael Whitehouse collection]

A train pauses just south of Wetton Mill station with a train for Waterhouses. In the foreground is the Hoo Brook, from which the locomotives lifted water until the installations at Hulme End were completed. The photograph, again colourised, was taken by the North Staffordshire Railway's official photographer, Edwin Harrison, and published in 1907. Harrison was employed by the NSR on a commission basis and established photographic studios at a very early date in 1857 in Newcastle under Lyme, becoming the town's leading photographer. [Michael Whitehouse collection]

A double-headed bank holiday train around 1918 near Hulme End, using some of the transporter wagons adapted to carry passengers and all four carriages. [W.H. Whitworth, Michael Whitehouse collection]

J.B. Earle, now painted in the North Staffordshire Railway's less ornate livery of madder lake lined out with a single yellow line, stands in the L&M station at Waterhouses. The station was a simple affair with a single platform having a small wooden shelter situated alongside the standard gauge line and accessed from the sloping ramp at the end of one of its station platforms. [Michael Whitehouse collection]

The 1.25pm Wednesdays and Saturdays only train for Waterhouses stands at Hulme End on Wednesday 11th July 1928 behind *E.R. Calthrop*, now in lined LM&SR crimson lake livery. The wagon on the transporter is a 10-ton coal wagon from the Buxton coal merchants Kirkland & Perkin, who had a sales office in the railway's goods yard at Hulme End. Coal traffic on the railway formed a substantial part of the freight carried, together with milk, and further standard gauge coal wagons can be seen in the goods yard behind the station nameboard. [A.W. Croughton, Michael Whitehouse collection]

E.R. Calthrop, with Tom Underwood at the regulator, pulls away from Ecton Creamery with two transporter wagons loaded with standard gauge milk tank wagons destined for the United Dairies Finsbury Park depot in London. From 1918 the railway carried this additional traffic which was to prove a lifeline. F.W. Gilbert Limited moved their dairy from Waterhouses to Ecton to secure larger premises by leasing the disused mine buildings which were enlarged to suit a dairy. A private siding was laid in the Ecton Creamery for loading milk churns and taking delivery of goods. The provision of this siding was quite a complex affair, requiring realignment of the running line and adding the siding from the existing loop. Milk production was of increasing importance during the First World War when farmers were being urged to help the war effort. The railway carried increasing numbers of 17-gallon milk churns throughout the war. In 1911 alone, approximately 220,000 gallons of milk were conveyed and by 1918 this had increased to 590,000 gallons. This required some modification to the transporter wagons to enable the railway to carry 4- or 6-wheel standard gauge vans. Later, modern, glass-lined milk tankers were transported to the new dairy and a cheese factory opened there. The creamery closed in 1932 and the railway lost its reason to exist. In the second photograph, Tom had added the transporter wagons to a mixed train already comprising another transporter with an SR open wagon loaded on it. In the background a 6-wheeled milk van can be seen sitting on a fourth transporter at the loading dock loaded with milk churns.
[Michael Whitehouse collection]

Arthur Dowler coals *J.B. Earle* on Hulme End shed on Friday 5th May 1933. Both coaling and ashing out the locomotives was a labour-intensive process, first offloading coal from wagons onto the stage, then loading ash from the firebox into the wagons. [MICHAEL WHITEHOUSE COLLECTION]

Both locomotives on shed at Hulme End on Saturday 22nd July 1933. *E.R. Calthrop* simmers outside whilst *J.B. Earle* is tucked up inside. Local historian and expert on the folklore of the L&M, Dr J.R. Hollick, reported that when *E.R. Calthrop* visited Crewe Works for periodic heavy repairs in 1929, it was returned to Waterhouses the wrong way round. Locomotives had always worked chimney first to Waterhouses on account of the fierce climb out of the valley. Running backwards up this incline increased fears of the firebox crown being uncovered as the water in the boiler surged towards the smokebox end of the boiler. The foreman at Hulme End urgently requested that the locomotive be sent back for turning. Crewe's reply was that the Hulme End depot had a perfectly good crane and so they should simply get on with it on home territory. The foreman was not having that, so *E.R. Calthrop* remained the wrong way round until its next visit to Crewe. For some reason *E.R. Calthrop* does not seem to have been used anywhere as much as *J.B. Earle*, whichever way round it happened to be facing. [MICHAEL WHITEHOUSE COLLECTION]

E.R. Calthrop stands at Waterhouses with a train for Hulme End on Saturday 22nd July 1933. The locomotive is the 'wrong way round' but, with only a month's service left in it, it was still sent to Crewe Works for minor repairs and was then returned the 'right way round'. [A.W. Croughton, Michael Whitehouse collection]

This photograph of *J.B. Earle* in LM&SR plain black livery on 29th April 1933 clearly shows the elegant colonial design of the Kitson 2-6-4Ts constructed at its Airedale Foundry. Both locomotives were ordered on 6th August 1903 and cost £1,725 each. The driving wheels were 2ft 6 inch in diameter with only a 6ft wheelbase; the 2-wheeled front radial truck enabled these locomotives to run round sharp curves in safety and with ease. The outside cylinders measured 11ft 6 inches diameter by 16 inch stroke, providing steam to the boiler set at 150lbs per sq. inch.
[H.C. Casserley, Michael Whitehouse collection]

I found Hulme End station as we turned a corner of the road, two miles from the village of Hartington. The railway rejoices in the name of the Leek & Manifold Valley Light Railway. This was inscribed on a brass plate on the steam locomotive which was hissing softly when I arrived to let the driver know all was well and ready for the start.

The driver, meanwhile, was sitting on the kerbstone, which marks the difference between the platform and the railway, reading his morning paper. He was a cheery soul, with very blue eyes and white teeth and he enjoys his railway, I am quite sure of that.

At one time he told me, the railway was the 'Milky Way' of the district. Hundreds of gallons of milk were carried from its little stations to the main line. Now, there is no great distribution of milk, but Manchester hikers love the railway, and so do the holiday parties, who leave their charabancs at Hulme End and do the railway trip while the cars proceed by a longer road to Waterhouses, and there pick them up.

About 500 holiday makers, mostly from the Potteries, travel on this line on August Bank Holiday. Then there are three trains a day, one in the morning, the next at 1pm and the third at 4pm. I booked for the lunchtime train and had three companions: a lady, a gentleman and a little boy.

There was an air of great peace over the station until about 12.50pm, when everyone seemed to get busy at once. The station master and a porter suddenly remembered about a load of coal and a couple of carriages which should be elsewhere, so the driver got busy and his mate began hunting these obstacles.

At 1.20pm we were off down the valley of the lost rivers. The carriage was divided into first and third class. There was a slight difference in the upholstery and, as the locomotive ran backwards on this journey, the first class got more smoke, which didn't really matter as we were all third class passengers.

I watched the beauties of the Manifold Valley; softly rounded hills, with wooded slopes, a river with crystal clear water, a profusion of wild flowers. We passed a field where a snow white tent shone in the sun, and we rolled along in the heart of the valley.

The driver ignored the stations on the way out; we passed Ecton (for Warslow) almost before I noticed it. Several of the stations were not marked by buildings, merely by signs, and others are important enough to have sheds for shelter. Butterton was next, and then a tunnel. Then, Wetton Mill, where children with bouquets of forget-me-nots waved to us from a nearly field.

Somewhere near here I noticed that we no longer saw the river, only a dry watercourse which we crossed and recrossed for the rest of the way. Dry, dusty stones looked hot in the sun, plantations spread their shade over the dry river and, here and there, tufts of grass and dried moss were on the rounded stones, while the well built stone bridges looked quite out of place and useless. We came to Redhurst Crossing. In front I saw hills grow higher and lose their roundness. A sharp peak towered above us and we reached Thor's Cave, which was high up on the left. Then we came to Grindon, then to Beeston Tor, then to Sparrowlee, and we were running out of the valley to see a wider sweep of the country.

We had to cross a main road and that took time, as the fireman got down and closed the gates against the traffic. After he had climbed back onto the locomotive, we moved on a little, then the guard re-opened the gates and climbed back into the carriage. We moved on again and in a minute or two drew up at Waterhouses, where the railway finds its big brother, the Leek railway.

Rumour has it that this line is to be closed. The railway will go on: the locomotive puffs its way with its load of carriages and passengers, sometimes half a dozen, sometimes a hundred. But the Manifold Valley is lovely and mysterious, with its unknown railway and lost rivers.

[B. Casson & Jean Thorburn]

E.R. Calthrop heads a demolition train in May 1937, comprising the long transporter, a short transporter and bogie goods wagon north of Dale Bridge at Ecton during track lifting by the scrap merchant Cohen, assisted by LM&SR platelayers. By the time track lifting work began, the railway's watering facilities had already been dismantled, so a portable pump and motor was mounted in front of the locomotive's smokebox in order that water could be taken from streams along the line. [STANLEY J. RHODES, MICHAEL WHITEHOUSE COLLECTION]

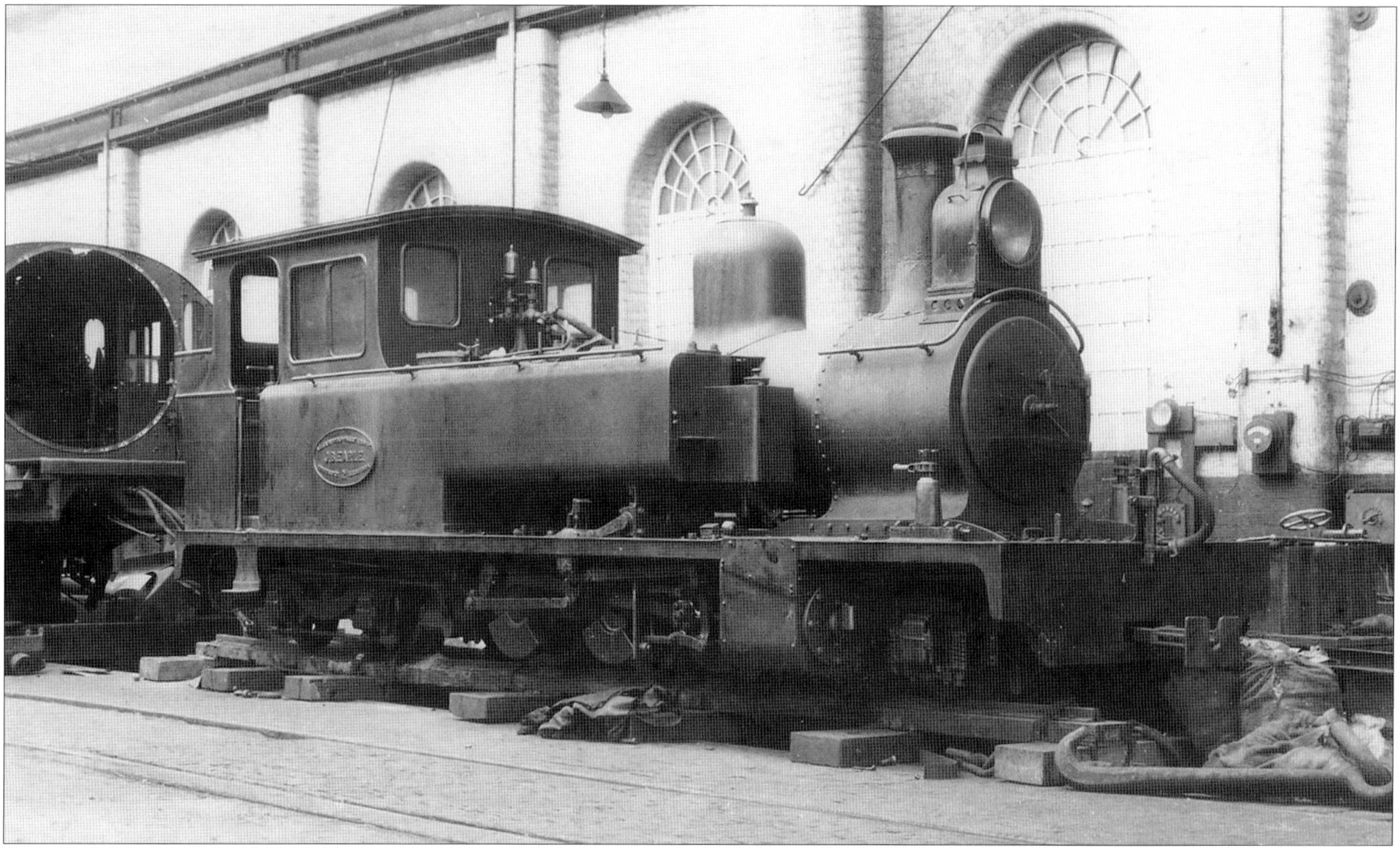

J.B. Earle was stored at the LM&SR's Crewe Works in 1935 in anticipation of a possible sale which did not materialise. She was scrapped in 1937. [MICHAEL WHITEHOUSE COLLECTION]

THE HUNSLET ENGINE CO. LTD *Engineers* LEEDS ENGLAND

2-6-0 TYPE
SIDE TANK ENGINE

Gauge of Railway	3 ft. 0 in.
Size of Cylinders	13 in. dia. × 18 in. stroke
Dia. of Coupled Wheels	3 ft. 0½ in.
,, Bogie Wheels	2 ,, 0 ,,
Rigid Wheelbase (Engine)	8 ,, 9 ,,
Total Wheelbase (Engine)	15 ,, 7 ,,
Height from Rail to Top of Chimney	10 ,, 9 ,,
Extreme Width	7 ,, 4½ ,,
Heating Surface—Small Tubes	494 sq. ft.
Firebox	66 ,,
Total	560 ,, 560 sq. ft.
Grate Area	9·75 ,,
Working Pressure	140 lbs. per sq. in.
Tank Capacity	750 gallons
Fuel Space (Coal)	13 cwts.
Weight Empty (Engine)	25 tons 5 cwts.
,, in Working Order (Engine)	30 ,, 15 ,,
Tractive Effort at 75 per cent. of Boiler Pressure	8750 lbs.
Minimum Radius of Curve Engine will traverse with ease	250 ft.
Weight per Yard of Lightest Rail advisable	40 lbs.
Load Engine will haul on Level	455 tons
,, ,, ,, up Incline of 1 in 100	225 ,,
,, ,, ,, ,, ,, ,, 1 in 50	125 ,,

Code Word—**TRELA**

Tralee & Dingle Railway 2-6-0T No. 2 shown within a Hunslet catalogue entry as a standard type offering, using the code name 'Trela'. Whilst a very successful design for this rugged 3ft gauge Irish railway, no examples of this type were built for any other line.

11
ENGLISH LOCOMOTIVE MANUFACTURING FOR THE WORLD:
THE HUNSLET ENGINE COMPANY

[Edited and abridged from L.T.C. Rolt's *Hunslet Hundred* book]

Until now, we have mainly considered the English narrow gauge from the domestic viewpoint. Apart from some notable industrial concerns, most of these operations were unsuccessful in the long run. The Hunslet Engine Company, on the other hand, was a spectacular success for over a hundred years by ensuring it was progressive, forward looking, acquisitive and reached out to the world for business; very largely due to the foresight and determination of Edgar Alcock, managing director, Hunslets were very lucky to have him, Over time, as Hunslets expanded, it took over other famous locomotive manufacturers such as Kerr, Stuart, Avonside, Manning, Wardle and Kitson. Early on it realised that the diesel engine was the future motive power and invested in it.

The Hunslet Engine Company was founded in Leeds in 1864. By then, half a lifetime had passed since the greater part of Britain's complex railway system had been built and British industry was then exporting steam locomotives all over the world. Yet the story of this one company and its craftsmen is closely linked by many fascinating threads of association with narrow gauge railways and the whole story of railways and locomotives from its earliest beginnings, inspiring a proud tradition of fine craftsmen.

By virtue of that great pioneer Matthew Murray, Leeds disputes with Newcastle the proud distinction of being the birthplace of the steam locomotive and demonstrates that our steam railways began as narrow gauge. Whilst Trevithick's designs built in Gateshead and South Wales demonstrated for the first time that this new form of traction was practicable, they did no more than demonstrate this fact because their weight was too great for the brittle cast iron horse tramways of the period. To overcome this difficulty some combination of light weight with high tractive power was needed and it was to this end that John Blenkinsop of Leeds patented his system of rack propulsion in 1811. Blenkinsop was not himself an engineer, so he entrusted the design and construction to Matthew Murray at the Round Foundry, although Trevithick was paid a royalty. The crude tramway along which Murray's locomotives first hauled their trains of coal wagons in 1812 passed almost within a stone's throw of the Hunslet works and ran on a narrow gauge of 4ft 1 inch. Until strong wrought iron rails were perfected, Blenkinsop's design with rack drive was the right answer for use on cast iron rails and Murray's locomotives proved capable of hauling 94 tons on the level at 3 $^1/_2$mph, no mean achievement in 1812. The Hunslet works was built on the site of an earlier locomotive works which was founded by an apprentice of Murray's, so the thread of tradition can be traced back unbroken to the earliest days of the pioneers.

Hunslets built locomotives for practically every country in the world, locomotives of every conceivable size and type, ranging from a pigmy narrow gauge locomotive for a Welsh quarry to an 8-coupled giant for China. Its locomotive registers included almost every variation upon the basic theme of the steam locomotive that the ingenuity of man has conceived: tram engines, steam railcars, geared locomotives, Fell engines, rack locomotives, Fairlie and Meyer articulated locomotives and even supreme oddities such as the Lartigue monorail engines built for the Listowel & Ballybunion Railway in Ireland.

The worksplate of the last South African Railways' Hunslet Taylor Garratt 2-6-2+2-6-2 to be built, in 1968.
[MICHAEL WHITEHOUSE COLLECTION]

All this rich past means pride in workmanship and represents a deep well of practical experience which can be drawn upon in solving the problems of the present. In these respects, tradition is an excellent thing for which there is no substitute. Yet a long tradition has its dangers and can easily introduce complacency. But Hunslet looked ahead to embrace the diesel engine from as early as 1920 and so prolonged its life. The moral is that tradition, properly regarded, is like an endless ladder presenting a perpetual challenge to the climber, but upon which it is fatal to stand still. It is not a flight of steps with a comfortable seat at the top.

The number of locomotives produced steadily increased requiring expansion to the works facilities: the erecting shop was expanded and new machine and boiler shops built together with a pattern and copper shops. The locomotive output became increasingly varied in size and type. From 1885, the works plan reflects a growing export business and the appearance of a stripping shop where locomotives were prepared for shipment

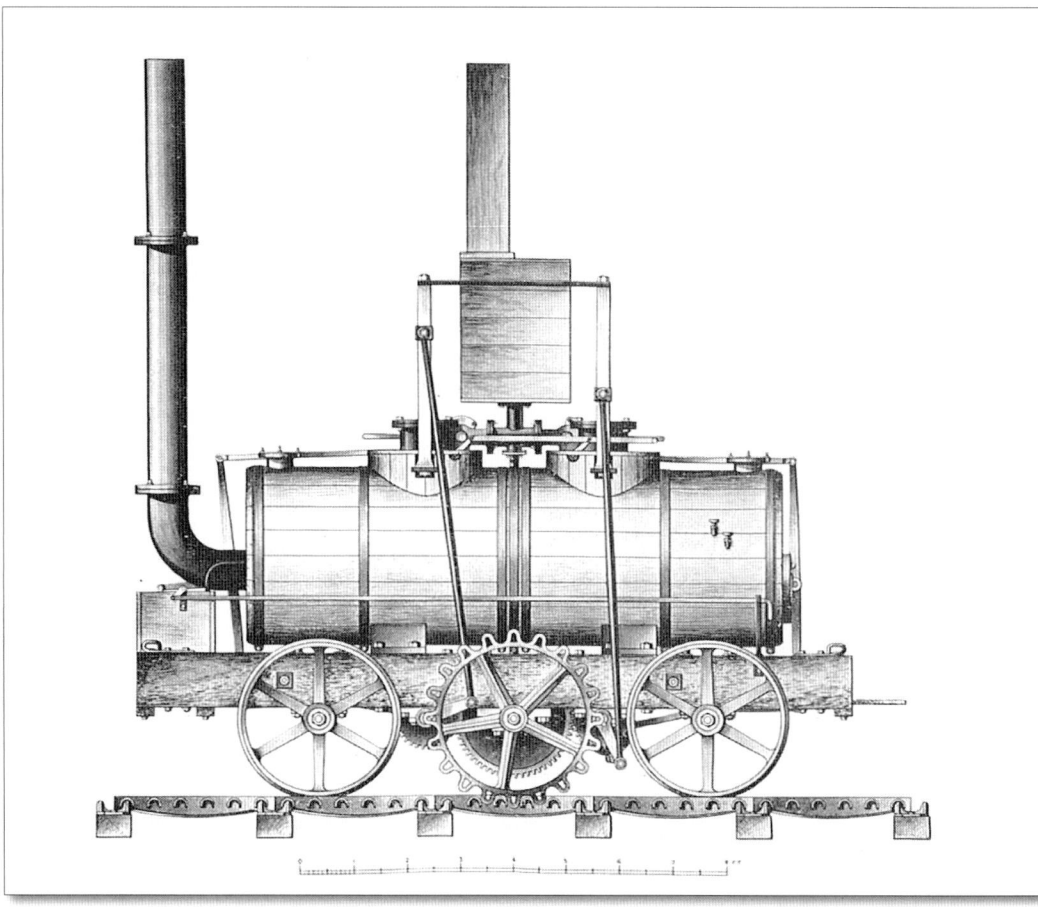

Salamanca was the first commercially successful steam locomotive, built in 1812 by Matthew Murray of Holbeck, for the edge-railed Middleton Railway between Middleton and Leeds, and predating Stephenson's Rocket by seventeen years. Named after the Duke of Wellington's victory at the Battle of Salamanca which was fought that same year, *Salamanca* was also the first rack and pinion locomotive, using John Blenkinsop's patented design for rack propulsion. A single rack ran outside the 4ft 1 inch narrow gauge tracks and was engaged by a large cog wheel on the left side of the locomotive. The cog wheel was driven by twin cylinders embedded into the top of the centre-flue boiler. The class was described as having two 8 inch × 20 inch cylinders, driving the wheels through cranks. The piston crossheads slid in guides, rather than being controlled by a parallel motion linkage like the majority of early locomotives. The engine saw twenty years of service; quite remarkable for a pioneering design.

abroad. Hunslet's catalogue well describes its activities:

'Engines for shipment to foreign countries are, after completion and trial in steam, dismantled carefully. All bright parts are then coated with anti corrosive varnish, or a mixture of white lead and tallow (easily cleaned off by turpentine or naphtha rubbed on with waste) and packed in zinc lined, water tight cases. All other parts are packed in cases rendered water tight by marine glued joints.

All cases are stoutly battened and hooped with iron. Boilers, frames, tanks etc., are boarded and protected by battens.

Special attention is given to the distinct marking of all parts for re-erection, and with all shipments we supply fully detailed lists of the contents of each package and case.'

As business continued to grow, a new and larger erecting shop was built so that, by the turn of the century, the company could cater for all its needs except castings (which were supplied by Manning, Wardle) and also despatch locomotives complete.

At this time the normal working day began at 6am and ended at 5.30pm. On raw winter mornings and at nightfall we must picture the smoky, clangorous gloom of the workshops lit only by oil lamps, by the tallow dips of the boiler makers and erectors, by the red glow of forges and rivet hearths or the sudden orange glare as a big heat was drawn from the furnace and swung under the tup of the tall steam hammer. Only over certain machines and above the workbenches of the joiners and pattern makers were gas lamps installed.

By now, the list of extras or modifications had reached impressive proportions, reflecting both the growth of the company's export trade and the technical evolution of the steam locomotive. It included such refinements as Westinghouse or automatic vacuum brakes, steam sanding gear, liquid fuel equipment, condensing apparatus and offers to meet a great variety of special needs in the form of cow catchers, American style headlamps, motion screens to comply with steam tramway regulations, steam water lifters and spark arrestor chimneys for wood burners.

In the old railway foundry days, responsible engineering opinion held that steam traction on a gauge substantially narrower than 4ft 8 1/2 inches was not a practical proposition. But one year before the Hunslet Engine Company was founded, the pioneer Festiniog Railway in North Wales converted their horse tramway to locomotive haulage and conclusively proved that steam traction was perfectly practicable even on a gauge so narrow as 1ft 11 1/2 inches wide. This successful experiment attracted world wide attention and quickly led to the widespread adoption of narrow gauge locomotives not only for private quarry and other industrial lines, but also for public railways both at home and abroad. At home, and especially in Ireland, narrow gauge railways later received a fresh fillip when the British Government authorised their construction under the simpler sanction of Light Railway Orders and waived costly Private Bill procedure. It can thus be anticipated that a firm intending to specialise in the construction of the lighter and smaller types of locomotive could scarcely have been born at a more propitious moment in railway history and the Hunslet Engine Company was quick to take advantage of this stroke of good fortune.

The company built its first narrow gauge locomotive in 1870: a 4-wheeled saddle tank Dinorwic which was delivered to

English Locomotive Manufacturing for the World: The Hunslet Engine Company

Charlie, one of a series of simple but very effective locomotives built for the Dinorwic Slate Quarry and also the nearby Penrhyn Quarry. Various slightly different designs were delivered over the years and the type has proved very popular in preservation, as it is a manageable small locomotive for an individual to own, maintain and run.

Hunslet's standard 4-6-0T designed for the War Office to be used on lightly laid, 60cm gauge, 20lb rail to take supplies and munitions up to the front line. Here seen with a group of American army service men on the Western Front in the First World War.

Gowrie, an 0-6-4T of a 'single' Fairlie design, built for the nominal 2ft gauge Welsh Highland Railway in 1908. This locomotive had a short life as the WHR itself did not survive. *Gowrie* has been described as an unsuccessful locomotive, but this type were popular in the USA. A replica is under construction, and it may yet be that Hunslet's design will be vindicated when we see this operating.

A standard Hunslet design of 0-6-0T, assembled for the 3ft 6 inch gauge Lagos Government Railway, Nigeria, seen here at Lagos port.

English Locomotive Manufacturing for the World: The Hunslet Engine Company

The author came across *Dom Carlos* unexpectedly in steam at the port at Lobito, Angola in 1973. This handsome but simple 3ft 6 inch 0-6-0T was supplied by Hunslet in 1905 for the Caminos de Ferro de Angola, built in a mere twenty-one days and, at the time of the author's visit, was still in use for its designed purpose. [MICHAEL WHITEHOUSE COLLECTION]

the quarry of the same name at Lanberis and was the first of twenty similar locomotives supplied to the same quarry. By 1902 the company had built locomotives to no less than fifteen different gauges and Hunslet locomotives were at work in thirty one countries scattered all over the globe. To meet the needs of these overseas railways, locomotives of greater variety in design were built. It soon became obvious that for the growing overseas market the company must be prepared to supply tender locomotives where the length of haul between fuelling points was very long or where wood fuel was to be used.

In its specialised field of the smaller and lighter types of locomotives, the craftsmen of the Hunslet works were past masters, as they showed in 1905 when they built a 3ft 6 inch gauge 0-6-0T *Dom Carlos* for Angola in a mere twenty one days from date of order to shipment. The order was received on 15th April; the plates were ordered and were all received by 25th April; the cylinder castings arrived from the foundry on 22nd. On the last day of the month the boiler was completed and tested and it was installed in the frames that night. On 5th May the locomotive was completed and painted. It was tested under steam the next day by which time the paint was dry. By 9th May it had been completely stripped and packed in cases ready for despatch and at 4am on the morning of 10th May it was alongside ship in Liverpool docks ready for loading.

But by now conditions in the locomotive trade were changing rapidy. The heyday of railway construction was over, the pace of expansion had slowed and as it did so the locomotive industry became more keenly competitive. Another very marked trend was that railways everywhere, irrespective of gauge, began to call for larger and more powerful locomotives as train weights increased. The days when the firm could afford to specialise in the lighter types of locomotive were over. In order to satisfy the needs of old overseas customers or to attract new ones they must be prepared to build larger and much heavier locomotives.

This change of policy first becomes significantly evident in the Engine Book in 1911 which included 2ft 6 inch gauge 2-8-0 tender engines for South America and, in 1912, two 2-8-4T locomotives for the Antofagasta, Chile & Bolivia Railway. The works was reorganised so that the demands of overseas railways for motive power of much more formidable proportions could be met. But demand for small locomotives persisted, especially on the outset of the First World War when the company produced a great number of small 60 cm 4-6-0T locomotives for the War Office, all specially designed with a very light axle load for use on the 20lb rails used for temporary tracks laid behind the fighting lines for bringing up munitions and stores.

In common with very many other businesses, when the war ended, Britain's locomotive builders faced considerable problems and the fortunes of individual builders during the ensuing twenty years depended to a great extent on the energy and resource with which these were met and overcome. Overseas trading connections had to be re-established but,

Hunslet built several 2ft 6 inch gauge 0-6-2Ts for the Nepal Railway between 1949 and 1962. This picture shows one of the type, Works No. 3875, on test at Hunslet's Leeds works on its multi-gauge track in 1962. [Dave Waldren collection]

Opposite page: Even the *Eagle* comic featured a Hunslet design locomotive in its pages. This boys' comic was well known for its 'exploded diagrams' of engineering subjects designed to educate its readers. On this occasion they featured the 2ft 6 inch 0-6-2T designed for Nepal and featured as a Narrow Gauge Locomotive for export. What finer accolade could there be for the English narrow gauge?! [Michael Whitehouse collection]

Above: The last Hunslet steam engine and the very last steam locomotive built for commercial service by a British company. Trangkil No. 4 built in 1971 to a Hunslet standard 0-4-2T 'Brazil' design for the 2ft 6 inch gauge Indonesian Trangkil sugar mill at Pati in central Java. The locomotive is seen here on test at Hunslet. It is now repatriated and works on the Statfold Barn Railway, albeit regauged to 2ft. [Dave Waldren collection]

Narrow-Gauge Locomotives FOR EXPORT

Although King Steam no longer reigns supreme in Britain, steam locomotives are still being built here for overseas markets. Nepal (noted for its Ghurkas, and within whose frontiers lies Mount Everest) has recently taken delivery of two British-made narrow-gauge tank locomotives, one of which is shown here.

These rugged little engines were built by the Hunslet Engine Company Ltd., of Leeds. They are comparatively simple in design, being non-superheated with a boiler pressure of 160 lb. per square inch, and are built for service on a 2 ft. 6 in.-rail gauge. Their short-coupled wheelbase of 6 ft. 2 in. permits them to traverse curves of 120-ft. radius quite comfortably. Weighing 24¼ tons in working order, they have a pulling power of 6,413 lb. (at 75 per cent. boiler pressure) which allows them to haul a load of 330 tons on the level.

Worthy of note is the fact that the Hunslet Engine Company, besides having a world-wide reputation for fine steam locomotives, were among the pioneer builders of Diesel shunters for use in Britain.

KEY TO NUMBERED PARTS

(1) Coal bunker, 25 cwt. capacity. (2) Side tanks, each holding 275 gallons of water. (3) Outer casing of dome. (4) Fire-box. (5) Fire-tubes. (6) Inner steam dome. (7) Two Ross 'pop' safety valves. (8) Steam regulator valve, operated by regulator handle (9), and feeding the cylinders through main steam pipe (10). (11) Injectors (one each side), feeding water from the tanks into the boiler through the clack valves (12). (13) Cylinders – two 10½-in. diameter x 16-in. stroke. (14) Piston. (15) Crosshead. (16) Connecting-rod. (17) Six-coupled driving wheels, 2 ft. 9 in. in diameter. These are inside the main frames (18) with their cranks (19) extended outside the frames. (20) Driving wheel springs. (21) Walschaert valve gear, controlled by the reversing handle in the quadrant (22), through the linkage (23). (24) Steam chest and slide-valves. (25) Branched blast pipe, carrying exhaust steam from cylinders. (26) Cylinder drain-cocks and operating linkage. (27) Sand boxes. (28) Trailing bogie. (29) Electric 300 watt. 10-in. headlamps, fitted to front and rear of locomotive. (30) Steam-driven turbo-generator, supplying current for headlamps. (31) Whistle. (32) Wooden roof to cab. (33) Combined coupling and buffing gear. (34) 'Cowcatcher' fitted to front and rear of locomotive. (35) Flexible brake connecting pipe.

owing to manufacturers turning to meet the war needs and changing production priorities, it took some time to get back to normal. During this time, some overseas railway companies and manufacturers stepped up their domestic production. British labour costs had doubled and considerable investment was needed to rebuild plant and machinery. If Hunslet was to regain its prominent place in the world of railways it was essential that production methods be greatly improved in order to reduce labour costs. Proposals for improvement were sanctioned by the board within nine days of being received; no doubt the order for twenty-six 4-6-0 superheated tender locomotives for the Indian State and South Indian metre gauge railways focused their minds. These improvements proved most worthwhile and more orders quickly followed from Ceylon, South America and for Burmese metre gauge 4-6-4Ts; all also generating further repeat orders.

Manning, Wardle, until now a friendly competitor, had failed to modernise and went into liquidation with the goodwill being acquired by Kitson but with Hunslet buying a portion of their workshops, enabling a further extension of its machine shop. In 1929 the innovations of oxy-acetylene flame cutting and electric arc welding changed and speeded up production methods. Although the thirties brought a decade of financial stringency and retrenchment, as the Hunslet works had been brought up to date and production methods improved, they were able to ride the great economic storm in which many a fine old firm foundered: Kerr, Stuart and Avonside went to the wall but Hunslets were able to purchase the goodwill and manufacturing rights of these two great firms, thus also inheriting the history and tradition which they had built up over the years. This immediately enabled Hunslet to execute repeat orders and spare parts for these designs from these two companies, especially as it now also had their drawings, patterns and blocks. Hunslet also developed the good working relationship which Kerr, Stuart had with Robert Hudson & Co. of Leeds, eventually giving rise to a range of light diesel locomotives.

During the 1930s, by far the most significant event in Hunslet's development was the introduction of the diesel locomotive and its rapid rise to popularity. This was all the more remarkable as it began during a period of acute industrial depression. This required great courage in the early 1930s to venture into such new and untried fields. This was due to the presence of mind and determination of Edgar Alcock, managing director, who had masterminded the changes in production since the First World War. His son John was brought into the business and told by his father that his job in life would be the development of the internal combustion engine locomotive and that he should educate himself at school and university accordingly. He was wisely encouraged to travel, and by visiting trade fairs all over the Continent he was able to study at first hand many new machines and methods. In 1928 father and son set out together on a long Continental tour which included visits to the works of every large locomotive builder in Germany, Italy and Switzerland. It was an experience of the greatest possible value.

The purchase of the goodwill of Kerr, Stuart & Co. in 1930 provided another golden opportunity. Kerr, Stuart had developed a range of light diesel locomotives fitted with McLaren-Benz engines, of which two, a 60 hp narrow gauge engine and a 90 hp standard gauge machine, were brought to Leeds from Stoke. Various improvements were made and, after several trials and tribulations, English Electric won an order for the prototype LMS standard gauge shunting locomotive with its electric transmission. Despite this setback, Hunslet persevered with their diesel mechanical design and with success. In 1934, they built an interesting locomotive for the 18ft gauge Woolwich Arsenal Railway (referred to in the *Minimum Gauge* essay) which was the first articulated diesel to be built by the company. The 75 hp engine drove a two speed gearbox from which the drive was transmitted to the two 4-wheeled bogies through jointed propeller shafts, bevel gears and jackshafts. The maximum tractive effort of this engine was 6,570lbs, yet the axle load was only 3 tons 19 cwt and a 30ft radius curve could be negotiated.

As far as Hunslet was concerned, the diesel locomotive had arrived. Each year an increasing number were laid down so that by the time of the outbreak of World War Two, steam and diesel production was approximately equal. These Hunslet diesels ranged in size and power from a little 10-12 hp contractor's locomotive to a 6-coupled metre gauge engine for Peru developing 242 hp. A Hunslet development during this period, second only in importance to that of the diesel locomotive itself, was the underground mines locomotive.

The Second World War witnessed a second switch over of British industry to war production in the 20th century. Although the emphasis was then turned to armaments, locomotives were still produced, including the new standard gauge 'Austerity' 0-6-0ST. After the war had ended, once again the company realised that it must put all efforts into expansion and development if the company was to meet the challenges of the post war years and, whilst various diversifications were embarked up, locomotive building still reigned supreme.

New developments were overseas and, perhaps Hunslet's long and distinguished manufacturing business ended with two distinct narrow gauge 'hurrahs'.

In April, 1949 Hunslet Africa (Pty) Ltd was formed with the object of manufacturing locomotives in the South African Transvaal. The manufacturing capacity was provided by the local firm of C.C. Taylor & Co. (Pty) Ltd and, from this works, the first African built Hunslet locomotives were commissioned with the 500th locomotive being completed in January, 1958. Hunslet, Taylor, as it became, completed their final two foot gauge 2-6-2+2-6-T Garratt locomotive for the Natal narrow gauge lines in 1968 – the same year as British Railways determined to finish with steam. These powerful and highly successful locomotives powered heavy sugar beet trains on five narrow gauge lines for many years to great effect. Several of their type have been imported to Wales where they now run passenger trains over the Welsh Highland and Vale of Rheidol Railways.

Hunslet's last order for a steam locomotive was for a 2ft 6in. gauge 'Brazil' design 0-4-2ST for the Indonesian Trangkil sugar mill at Pati in central Java. Probably this order for a single locomotive came as a surprise to everyone, but it was duly executed. Hunslet concluded its steam locomotive manufacturing business in style with a last order for a simple standard locomotive type, easily and quickly built 'off the shelf'. Fortunately, when this locomotive finished its useful life, Graham Lee, the founder of the Statfold Barn Railway, re-imported the locomotive, regauged it to 2ft and now everyone can see this wonderful 'last of the line' for themselves.

12
THE LAST STEAM WORKED SYSTEM:
THE BOWATERS PAPER RAILWAY

William Vansittart Bowater was reputed to be ill-tempered, tyrannical and hard-drinking. These traits led him to be dismissed by his first employer, James Wrigley & Sons, a Manchester papermaking firm. But by the time he was 43 years of age, in 1881, he had established his own business as a paper wholesaler in the City of London, the heart of the British newspaper publishing and printing industries.

The latter years of the 19th century saw the birth of the popular press in Britain and demand for newsprint, and so paper, soared. Bowater secured contracts with the *Daily Mail* and *Daily Mirror*, amongst others, his five sons joined him in business and so W.V. Bowater & Sons was all set to become the largest paper manufacturer in the country and took its first steps to become a multinational corporation.

Its first manufacturing base was at Northfleet, on the south side of the Thames Estuary near Gravesend, starting production in 1926. Armstrong, Whitworth & Co. Limited, well known for its railway locomotive production, built the company a paper mill, but did not make a good job of it. By now, the company was being run by the founder's grandson, Eric Bowater, who became Chairman & Managing Director and dominated the firm's affairs by the sheer force of his personality. He sorted out the Northfleet problems and expanded the firm further by the development of a further mill on the Mersey near Liverpool and the acquisition, in 1936, of paper mills at Sittingbourne and Kemsley from Edward Lloyd Limited, which doubled the firm's output of newsprint. By then, Bowaters was producing 60 per cent of British newsprint and had become the largest newsprint undertaking in Europe.

Of course, the part of the Bowater's empire we are interested in here is the transport system between the Edward Lloyd paper mills and Ridham dock on the River Swale. Lloyd acquired the site at Sittingbourne in 1863 for the storage of straw which was initially transported by water, to their mill at Bow. Lloyd then developed a paper mill at Sittingbourne itself in 1876 because of its good transport links with the rest of the country by water,

Kerr, Stuart 'Brazil' Class 0-4-2ST *Melior*, built in 1924. [Neil Parkhouse collection]

One of the Kerr Stuart 0-4-2STs stands on track just outside the mill in the early 1960s. The photographer wrote an article about the railway which appeared in the May 1964 issue of *Railway World*. [P.F. WINDING, COURTESY ROBERT HUMM]

The Last Steam Worked System: The Bowaters Paper Railway

A rare picture of the Bagnall 0-4-0T *Rattler* (Works No. 1978 of 1913), which was acquired from the Cape Copper Company of Briton Ferry, via the dealers George Cohen & Sons Ltd of Swansea, in 1942. Bought at a time of locomotive shortages, after starting to dismantle it for repairs, Bowaters apparently gave up as it was in such poor condition and it was scrapped by September 1949, some time after this picture was taken, on 9th August 1947.
[GEORGE ALLIEZ, COURTESY ANDREW NEALE]

road and rail, the latter being by the London, Chatham & Dover Railway. From 1867, transport was provided on Milton Creek, a narrow waterway navigable only by barges, with a wharf built at the Sittingbourne end. This wharf was connected to the paper mill by a 2ft 6 inch narrow gauge railway. This was worked, at first, by horses, but in 1904, Kerr, Stuart & Co. provided two of its Standard 'Brazil' design 0-4-2STs, followed by a third locomotive of the same design in 1908.

By then the Milton Creek facilities were proving inadequate and so, in 1913, Lloyd obtained powers to build a dock for ocean going ships at Ridham on the River Swale and extended the narrow gauge railway to it. The First World War intervened and the Admiralty took over the dock in 1917, built the standard gauge connection to the Sheerness branch at Swale Halt and used the facility as a Royal Naval salvage depot. But from 1919, Lloyd was able to restart operations. In 1924 he opened the Kemsley mill, also connected by railway which, by this time, extended to some 3½ miles of main line and about 10 miles of sidings. Apart from some siding alterations, the railway system then remained largely unchanged for the rest of its commercial existence until 1969. But the increases in business continued which led to the building of an overhead conveyor between Ridham dock and Kemsley mill, to ease pressure on the railway, and to carry logs from ships to the mill stockpile. The main traffic on the railway was wood pulp, china clay and finished paper.

New steam locomotives were added to stock and numbered 14 in all. These comprised four 0-4-2STs: *Leader, Premier, Excelsior, Melior*; six 0-6-2Ts: *Superior, Conqueror, Alpha, Triumph, Superb* and *Chevallier*; two fireless locomotives: 2-4-0 *Unique* and 0-4-0 *Victor*; an 0-4-0T *Rattler* and, lastly, an 0-4-4-0 Meyer design: *Monarch*. The railway also had a small diesel.

Traffic continued to operate, largely uninterrupted, during the Second World War. In 1954 a new locomotive maintenance depot was opened at Kemsley, fully equipped to undertake the heaviest repairs. An interesting feature of the railway was the free passenger train for Bowater's staff, which ran to a fixed timetable throughout the 24-hour working day with thirteen return workings between Sittingbourne and Ridham, including three trains which ran completely during the hours of darkness and one which was scheduled to reach Sittingbourne at midnight exactly! A unique train on the narrow gauge in the British Isles.

Although railway operations continued unabated, Bowaters was changing. Before the Second World War, the firm continued to grow, with international acquisitions in Scandinavia to secure its own pulp supplies, previously an area of vulnerability in its place in the paper supply chain. Wartime controls to divert

Monarch, a modified Meyer articulated 0-4-4-0T built by Bagnall in 1953, in the locomotive shed on 19th July 1958. *Monarch* was the last industrial narrow gauge steam locomotive built for use in the UK. Six similar locomotives were built for sugar estates railways in South Africa.
[DAVE WALDREN COLLECTION]

Bagnall 0-6-2T *Superb*, built in 1940. [Dave Waldren collection]

resources to the war effort had a devastating effect on Bowaters' UK newsprint production, demonstrating once again that unforeseen and uncontrollable events can significantly affect even a good business as well as destroying out of date ones, as we have read elsewhere in this book. Bowaters' Northfleet mill closed for paper production in 1973, but remained in operation for Bowater Scott for the production of toilet tissue. Bowaters diversified into paper packaging. Its American business grew, however, and by the mid-1950s, Bowaters was the largest producer of newsprint in the world. Acquisitions continued with the Mersey Paper Co. and even a shipping fleet, all with the objective of being as self-sufficient in the marketplace as possible. But this strategy was flawed. Competitors had also made substantial investments and from 1957 the market was over supplied; prices weakened, profits disappeared but borrowings still had to be serviced and repaid.

Management changes and diversification saved the day and, in 1984, the North American business was demerged and separated from the UK operations, but all this takes us beyond the all-important year in 1969, when Bowaters was in the midst of new management and making cost savings to tackle over capacity in the newsprint market. This was to affect the railway as time and motion consultants were engaged in 1965 to increase the efficiency of its paper making operations. One of their recommendations was to replace the narrow gauge railway by road transport.

Generally, within the company the closure was not a popular decision as the railway had become an institution and everyone was fond of it. Whilst Bowaters had never sought publicity for the railway, as interest in industrial railways grew and steam locomotive operation in Britain waned, the railway's fame spread. It became the last narrow gauge railway in the UK to be steam operated for an industrial use. Visits to the railway became a regular feature and Bowaters were content to entertain requests from railway societies to visit and travel over the line.

Fortunately, the board of directors recognised this interest and authorised the manager of the Kemsley mill to see if it would be possible to preserve some of the railway.

He approached Captain Peter Manisty, the then Chairman of the Association of Railway Preservation Societies who, in turn, contacted Malcolm Burton, Chairman of the Locomotive Club of Great Britain to ask if the Club might be interested. The answer was an emphatic 'Yes'!

A plan was conceived whereby Bowaters kept ownership of the land and railway and the LCGB were permitted to operate the line at a nominal rent as public attraction, but only from Sittingbourne to Kemsley, with the rest of the railway being abandoned. This section included the reinforced concrete viaduct, more than a quarter of a mile long and the major engineering feature of the railway. The Club acquired some of the locomotives and rolling stock, with others being dispersed to private collections and the Whipsnade and Umfolozi railway.

On 4th October, 1969 Mr T. Wilding, a Bowaters Director, handed over a licence agreement to enable the LCGB to begin operations and 0-6-2T *Triumph*, decorated with bunting and a special headboard hauled a special train to mark the occasion. Accepting the licence document, Mr J.C. Rogers, President of the LCGB, spoke warmly of the generous and public-spirited steps Bowaters were taking in the interests of steam enthusiasts everywhere. Even the Bowaters Chairman sent a message saying that he looked forward to visiting to 'play trains'. After the handover, guests were fittingly entertained to refreshments at the Kemsley Social Club.

Fireless 0-4-0 locomotive *Victor*, built in 1929 and scrapped in 1967, seen here in 1959. [DAVE WALDREN COLLECTION]

The railway was gradually developed as a tourist attraction and a separate company, the Sittingbourne & Kemsley Light Railway established to run the operation. Bowaters sold the mills in 1986 and paper production ceased entirely at Sittingbourne mill in 2007 and the railway was forced to cease operating by the then owners M-real. The British railway press reported that the last remaining narrow gauge industrial railway was highly likely to be no more. A sad day.

However, along with many other enthusiasts, I saw this announcement and thought closure would be such a sad event and wondered if something could be done about it. I reached for the phone and called the editor of *Steam Railway* magazine and asked to be put in touch with the S&KLR to see if they would like some pro bono legal assistance to try to broker a solution. They did.

As there was nothing to lose, having read a copy of their legal document on which their operation was based, I called M-real and asked to meet them. They acquiesced and what resulted was, in hindsight, really quite extraordinary. Simon Layfield from Rocks to Rail joined me to add his property expertise to my legal knowledge.

The best thing in such circumstances is first to listen. M-real volunteered that they wanted to clear the site and so sought to remove a bunch of enthusiasts playing trains who were in their way. They then asked me why I sought to intervene as, surely a hobby no longer had any place. I replied that I had offered to help as I thought it a shame the last remaining narrow gauge industrial railway should close, that the volunteers had made as good a fist of running it as a tourist attraction as they could and that, rather like Bowaters had, M-real should give them a leg up. They disagreed. So then I suggested the S&KLR had tenant's rights to be granted a new lease under the protection provisions of the Landlord & Tenant legislation as they had been in possession and operation for more than the requisite period of time. Now, simply by their body language, I could see M-real knew this, as clearly they too had taken legal advice. They retorted that they had set aside £25,000 to fight any such claim and that, as the S&KLR had no money, they would eventually win. This was Goliath speaking.

I quietly pointed out that, in my view, they would lose and explained why. M-real had not expected or anticipated these steps and so were off guard. I seized the further advantage and suggested that they formalise the arrangements in a lease and, moreover, that they donate the £25,000 they had earmarked to fight their corner to the railway to give them the leg up they needed! It quite quickly became clear that M-real could very largely achieve their objectives in land development with much of the railway remaining in place and so they agreed! All quite remarkable really and a proud achievement. The preserved railway was able to build on these initial foundations and Nick Mason enabled the establishment of SKLR Heritage resulting in finding the funding to buy the land from Sittingbourne viaduct station to just short of Kemsley Mill, take a 999 year lease on the majority of the remaining railway and a 25 year lease of the railway facility at Kemsley Mill.

The moral of the story is to take independent advice, do your research, behave firmly but reasonably and turn the tables as far as you can. Try it someday.

Bagnall 0-6-2T *Alpha*, built in 1932, photographed on 19th July 1958. [DAVE WALDREN COLLECTION]

Kerr, Stuart 0-4-2ST *Premier*, built in 1905, photographed on 17th December 1958. [DAVE WALDREN COLLECTION]

Bagnall 0-6-2T *Triumph*, built in 1934, photographed on 19th September 1958. [Dave Waldren collection]

Kerr, Stuart 0-6-2ST *Leader*, built in 1905, on 19th July 1958. [Dave Waldren collection]

One of the Bagnall 0-6-2Ts at Ridham Dock shunting a train load of paper bound for Norway by ship. [Dave Waldren collection]

The Last Steam Worked System: The Bowaters Paper Railway

Tourist special: Kerr, Stuart 0-4-2ST *Premier* of the S&KLR arrives at Sittingbourne with a train from Kemsley on 18th September 1971, crossing one of the first and largest reinforced concrete viaducts in the UK at 882 metres long and with 118 spans and 6 bridges. [G.D. KING]

English Electric battery locomotive No. 515 stands at Ridham Dock in 1960. It was nicknamed 'The Tank' and scrapped in 1969. Note the overhead conveyor system in the background. [GORDON EDGAR]

Bagnall 0-6-2ST, Conqueror, built in 1922, at Ridham Dock waiting with a train of bulk paper for loading. [Dave Waldren collection]

The 0-6-2T *Conqueror* stands at Ridham Dock. [DAVE WALDREN COLLECTION]

Alpha with a staff passenger train at Ridham Dock in May 1966. [GORDON EDGAR]

Kerr, Stuart 'Brazil' Class twins, *Premier* and *Excelsior*, sit in sunshine on shed at Sittingbourne. [GORDON EDGAR]

The 2-4-0 fireless locomotive, *Unique*, built by Bagnall in 1923, seen here photographed on 4th October 1969. [Dave Waldren collection]

Bagnall 0-6-2T *Alpha* with a train of loaded pulp wagons for Sittingbourne Mill at Ridham Dock in June 1966, with the trailing load being checked before departure. [Gordon Edgar]

Fireless 0-4-0 locomotive *Victor*, built by Bagnall in 1929, stands out of use at Kemsley Mill on 19th August, 1964. [JOHN COSFORD]

The 0-4-2ST *Leader* coming up the grade from Sittingbourne locomotive shed on 19th August 1964. [JOHN COSFORD]

Fireless 2-4-0 locomotive *Unique*, seen at work pushing a trainload of waste paper to the stacks at the rear of Kemsley Mill. [JOHN COSFORD]

ABOVE LEFT: Washed logs going up the shute to the pulping plant at Kemsley Mill on 19th August 1964. [JOHN COSFORD]

ABOVE RIGHT: The interior of one of the storage sheds at Ridham Dock filled with rolls of finished paper on 19th August 1964. [JOHN COSFORD]

RIGHT: An enormous log pile built up around one of the aerial ropeway support towers on 19th August 1964. [JOHN COSFORD]

LEFT: Bowaters' only internal combustion locomotive, Hunslet 0-4-0 diesel No. 4182, built in 1953, stands at Ridham Dock on 19th August 1964. [JOHN COSFORD]

Triumph and *Unique* stand back-to-back at Kemsley Mill in May 1966. Another huge stack of wood can be seen in the background waiting to be pulped. The worksplate on the far right is from the 0-4-2ST *Excelsior*. [GORDON EDGAR]

The railway running between high walls of bundled paper at Ridham Dock on 19th August 1964. [John Cosford]

The 0-6-2T *Chevallier* seen here standing by the paper stacks at Ridham Dock on 19th August 1964, was built by Manning, Wardle in 1915 and acquired second-hand from the Chattenden & Upnor Railway in 1950. This locomotive was larger than the Bagnall 0-6-2Ts and had a proper coal bunker behind the cab. [John Cosford]

Superb shunting the works passenger train at Ridham Dock on 19th August 1964. [John Cosford]

Triumph pushing a train of paper pulp near Kemsley Mill on 19th August 1964. [John Cosford]

Triumph, having crossed the standard gauge network on the level, pushes a loaded train of paper pulp up to the storage area at Kemsley Mill on 19th August 1964. [JOHN COSFORD]

0-6-2T *Superior* shunts a rake of mixed wagons alongside a Bowaters red-liveried AEC 8-wheeled, flat bed lorry at Kemsley Mill on 19th August 1964. Note the crane lorry just creeping into picture on the left. [JOHN COSFORD]

The way enthusiasts used to be able to travel before the introduction of the Health & Safety at Work Act, 1974! Teenagers from the Festiniog Railway Society stand at ease on an empty bogie flat wagon whilst journeying between Kemsley Mill and Sittingbourne on an enthusiast visit on 19th August 1964. The party were welcomed by Bowaters in the staff canteen with an outline of safety rules, then taken by the workman's passenger train to Ridham and allowed to wander around. They then walked to Kemsley Mill and rode on these flat wagons back to Sittingbourne. [JOHN COSFORD]

IN VOLUME 2:
**DEVON & CORNWALL INDUSTRIAL RAILWAYS,
WATERWORKS RAILWAYS,
LYNTON & BARNSTAPLE RAILWAY,
SNAILBEACH RAILWAY,
ASHOVER LIGHT RAILWAY,
WOLVERTON & STONY STRATFORD TRAMWAY,
JERSEY RAILWAY,
CHATTENDEN & UPNOR RAILWAY,
FURZEBROOK RAILWAY,
BEYER PEACOCK,
POST OFFICE RAILWAY,
EARLY PRESERVATION INITIATIVES.**